Stop Saying Yes to Mr. No Good

Get Toxic Men Out of Your Life Once and For All

Karlicia D. Lewis

Stop Saying Yes to Mr. No Good: Get Toxic Men Out of Your Life Once and For All
Copyright © 2013 by Karlicia Lewis

ISBN 978-0615833910

Printed in USA

Dedication

All honor goes to God, who is the only one that could have ever made writing this book possible. I owe Him my all. This book is dedicated to anyone who has ever been in a relationship that made them feel unappreciated, unloved, and disrespected. This is a dedication to all the women who know their self worth, as well as those who are struggling in the process of learning to love themselves. This is a dedication to all the women and men that I interviewed and surveyed throughout the process of writing this book. Last but not least, this book is dedicated to my family. I am blessed beyond measure to have such great role models in my life who have helped me learn the importance of loving myself. I am humbled, I am grateful. Thank you.

Table of Contents

Introduction

Whatever your reason may be for picking up this book let me first say congratulations to you! By reading this book, you are acknowledging that enough is enough, and you are ready to stop settling when you know that you deserve better, no matter what anyone else has to say. I applaud you for making a decision to weed the drama out of your life. No better time than the present!

The point of writing "Stop Saying Yes to Mr. No Good" was to help those that deal with men that don't treat them right. Many have adapted to a life of settling for anybody just to be able to say that they have a man. Many pretend to the public that they're happy with their partner, but deep down they're miserable. Some of them don't even have a clue as to why they're not happy, and some are simply in denial about what's going on in their relationship. This book will not only help you identify the behaviors you're not happy with, it will also help you in learning yourself, as well as taking control to ensure you get the happiness you deserve.

I hope that this will be a book that you can refer back to at any time to help reassure you that you are worth more than settling for someone that doesn't treat you right. Please don't be afraid to use this book as a relationship manual, as there are many checklists regarding your partner as well as yourself. This book serves as reassurance that you are not alone in your journey of learning to love yourself more, and settle less.

"Stop Saying Yes to Mr. No Good" is broken down into different sections that make up the complete process of getting out of an unhealthy situation and gaining happiness. Part 1 will discuss the no good man, breaking down the different types you may encounter, and the different kinds of women these guys normally go after. This section will help you in identifying the behaviors you may be experiencing, and will also help you understand why these behaviors continue to exist.

Part 2 is all about taking action. In this section, you will finally have the confidence and courage to get rid of the no good man (or men) in your life, once and for all. You will learn the importance of saying and meaning "no". You will learn how to deal with toxic men that continue to try to come back. This section will also help you to deal with the side effects of taking that major step to remove poisonous men from your life.

Part 3 will focus merely on you. In this section, we will discuss how important it is to be real with yourself, and how to accept the reality of your relationships. Part 3 helps you to understand the internal factors, which also play a major role in why we choose the partners we do. This section will also serve to enhance your self esteem, and help you to understand the importance of loving yourself completely before you can put your all into a relationship with another. After all, loving yourself (and the lack thereof) plays a major part in relationships with others.

Part 4 is all about starting fresh and enjoying being

free. In this section, you will take your newfound confidence for a spin! Take advantage of this time to create a new and improved lifestyle, as well as a new take on dating, now that you know exactly what you will and won't tolerate. Part 4 is all about celebrating a settle free life!

I am sure there will be many that take offense to me discussing and labeling no good men. Let me say that there are plenty of men out there who don't engage in behaviors such as the ones discussed in this book. If there weren't men out there worth giving a chance at all, then I would have no reason to be telling you to get rid of the toxic ones. This book is not about bashing men. It is about pinpointing the type that doesn't make you happy, and weeding them out so that you can make room for the one that will. Let me also say that this book is not just for women. The process of eliminating toxic men does not discriminate!

Are you ready for this life changing journey?

Tips to help you take full advantage of this book

Mr. No Good has been around since the beginning of time, and comes in many different packages. This type of man is the downfall of many relationships, and the breakdown of many women's self respect.

Definition of a no good man

You will hear a different definition of a no good man from each person you ask. This is because every situation is individualized. Sue may think no good men only cheat, while Mary may think cheating consists of being a man that beats on women. Everybody's idea of Mr. No Good will be customized, as well as their opinion of who makes the list.

I decided to come up with a pretty universal definition of Mr. No Good, based on my survey of various women across the country.

Mr. No Good: A male that engages in behaviors that harm their partner or the relationship, directly and/or indirectly

While we're at it, I'd also like to define the word "relationship", because many like to think that word can only be used when you and your partner have a title of "married", or "boyfriend and girlfriend".

relationship: any two (or more) individuals that communicate, and/or engage in some form of intimacy, whether it be long conversations, sex, texting, etc.

Examples: sex buddies, long distance lovers, husband and wife, boyfriends, girlfriends, lover and mistress, sugar daddy/sugar mama, etc.

I hope that these definitions make it easier for you to understand the concepts of this book.

I have classified many different types of no good men that you are most likely to encounter, or men that you have already experienced. The guy you are involved with may not have all the qualities listed. He may have different qualities that fall into different categories. Either way there are some important tips I will give you in navigating this section.

Be honest. This is so important, not just in this section, but throughout the whole book. Being honest will help you accurately pinpoint what kind of guy you are involved with. Honesty will make dealing with your own situation easier. Remember, this is your book and you don't have to share your findings about your relationship with anyone else. Don't lie to get the answers and explanations you want to hear. It defeats the purpose of taking this major step in your life. This book should not be read just for you to put it down and say nothing is wrong, knowing that there are issues. You are defeating yourself when you are in denial.

Don't make excuses. This will be a common problem for the readers of this book. Don't feel bad, you've spent a lot of time making excuses as to why you let certain things slide, so it's understandable that you would have a hard time changing that. But leave all the excuses at the door. You're not being judged, and there's no one here to turn their nose up or down at you, so you have no one to explain to but yourself. Forget about the how often and the why when answering questions about your partner. If the answer is yes, it's yes. If it's a no, it's no. I deliberately left blank lines out of this section. There is no need to explain away his behaviors, especially if it's just to blame yourself or others, which is probably what you were going to try to do (we've all been there).

Get out of denial and be smart. This may seem like common sense, but obviously none of us would ever stay dealing with a no good man if it was. It is very important to be smart about the findings. If you find yourself checking off many of the characteristics in one category, please don't be naïve enough to continue to disregard the obvious. The traits that I have listed for each type of toxic man are pretty common red flags. This tip can be tied into being honest with yourself.

Are you ready? Take a deep breath, and let's do this!

What I hope to get out of this book

_____
_____
_____
_____
_____
_____
_____

How I hope to feel after reading this book

_____
_____
_____
_____
_____

I feel that I could use a little help with my relationships in the category of

_____
_____
_____
_____
_____
_____
_____

Chapter 1-The Ladies Man

The Ladies' Man is definitely one that we find in almost every day of our lives. This is the guy that loves his single status, and takes complete advantage of it. He spends time with many different women, as well as sleeping with them. Juggling women is his specialty.

Mr. Ladies' Man comes in different forms. He can be the young guy that has never really had a long term relationship, or he can be an older guy who has been a player all his life. He can also be the guy that was married or always in relationships, and now he's just out to have fun with a variety of women. Mr. Ladies' Man can be well off financially, but he can also be unemployed. Let's be honest. Contrary to popular belief, there are men out there that are broke but still have a lineup of women.

Do any of these traits seem familiar?

- He's often too busy and explains that to you a lot
- You initiate calls and text more than he does
- He barely answers his calls, and sometimes doesn't even call you back
- He tells you he's just "chilling" or not looking for anything serious

- He lies, even about simple things
- He has a lot of female "friends"
- He works with a lot of females
- He has a great detailed explanation every time he messes up with you
- He tends to substitute things for time spent with you
- He doesn't introduce you to important people in his life , such as family

Now these traits can mean other things as well, but most of the time these behaviors show the obvious; he isn't willing to make the time he needs to. However, with the Ladies' Man, it may not be because he's not into you. It may be the fact that he's also digging other women he's dating, and he's awful at managing his time among his ladies. So don't focus on the possibility that he may not like you at all. The problem is that he's not into you enough to get rid of these other chicks that are cutting into your time, or what could be your time, if he wasn't such a ladies' man.

<u>He's too busy</u>

Mr. Ladies' Man knows that he has women already in his life, but due to the fact that he's single, he refuses to put a limit on it. So anytime he sees something he likes, he goes after it. Why? Because he can, and it's the very reason he's single. He has to find a way to split his free time with the women in his life, so that they won't complain, and won't cut him off. Knowing what he already has on his

13

plate, he lets you know upfront that he's a busy guy. Some guys may go into detail, talking about what keeps them busy, some may lie, and others will just simply keep it at "I'm a busy guy". The Ladies' Man knows that he can somewhat keep the ladies off of his back by telling them this, so that when he spends time with his other women, there won't be a major fuss about how he's spending his time. He already let you know ahead of time. A simple "I'm busy most of the time" can cover all bases. This is his way of being honest, yet keeping you out of his business.

Most men will say that their job keeps them busy. I'm sure you've heard this plenty of times, especially from one who works more than one job. Work is the excuse often used because they know that most women won't argue with that, nor will they try and verify if he's at work when he says he is.

He barely calls.

Moment of truth

- How often do you call/text him daily?
- How often is he the first to call you?
- How often does he respond to your calls/texts in a timely manner?
- Is his communication with you mainly him returning your calls/texts?

These questions may all seem to be asking the same thing, but they are each specific questions that will help you see clearly who is getting the short end of the stick.

The Ladies' Man normally has a pattern. He will usually be accessible in the beginning. He will not only answer calls and texts, but he will be the one doing most of the calling. Why? It's because you're a new addition to the team. You're something like a challenge, a mystery, and you bring the excitement of something new. The Ladies' Man is experienced enough to know that a woman goes crazy over a guy that shows major effort in getting to know her. They throw on the charm in great measures.

After a while, you probably noticed that the attention decreased. You found yourself calling and texting him more often. The first thought is usually "Did I do something wrong?" or "Did the sex change things?". Let's be honest: this is because giving it up too soon will definitely erase the thrill and challenge the Ladies' Man thrives on. We will discuss this later.

So you're wondering why you stopped hearing from him as much, and constantly talking to your girls trying to come up with a legitimate answer. The answer is quite simple, and comes down to 4 options.

A. He has met someone else, and is putting his time in with her because it's a new situation, like you once were.
B. He is spending more time with one of his females he had before you came into the picture.
C. He's rotating his options, and it's just not your turn.
D. He's lost interest, for whatever reason.

Notice I didn't add the option that he could be busy. **There's no such thing as being too busy to pick up a phone sometime within 24 hours to call someone you're interested in.** In 24 hours, there is always some kind of down time, no matter what profession you are in. When a person is interested, they make time to call you, because they want to talk to you, and they want you to know that you are on their mind. The same way he was making time for you in the beginning is the same time he can - and should-continue to make.

PAY ATTENTION

Here's a little assignment the next time you're spending time with Mr. Ladies' Man. Pay attention to the following things:

- Does he put his phone on silent?
- Does he send and check messages?
- Does he just let his phone ring?
- Does he press ignore on calls?
- Does he step outside to make phone calls?

These are common signs that he may have someone else in his life that he is spending time with. While he's respectful enough to avoid speaking with his women in front of you, make sure that you are not blind to the reality that you aren't his only interest.

He only texts you

This is a major practice of Mr. Ladies' Man. They can easily keep all their women satisfied by texting. **Texting can be his way of keeping you happy while he's spending time or talking to another woman** .He may not be answering his phone, because he may be entertaining another woman, but because he doesn't want to upset you or any of his other women, he will text. It makes the women calling feel a little better because he responded, even though he could be in bed or on a date with another woman. Meanwhile, the woman he is with at the time isn't getting upset either, because he can pretend he's texting a family member, friend, child's mother, coworker etc. I'm sure you've run into this kind of behavior before.

Texting does not constitute a good relationship. So many are pleased with getting texts, or holding long text conversations with their partner, but you shouldn't be, for many reasons.

Texting is very informal. When you're interested in someone, you want to know more about them, and you want to spend time with them. Talking on the phone or in person is more personal. There's more of a genuine feel to an actual conversation, no matter how good a text message makes you feel. Text messages can only say so much to convey emotions. It's also easier for someone to lie or have their messages misconstrued through texts. I'm sure you're familiar with those moments of having to send 5 or more messages just to get your point across, and being frustrated when you get only a short text reply, or no response at all.

Texting takes more effort than picking up a phone to call. If you are going to sit and text someone for longer than two rounds of messages, you obviously have a lot to say and need to be having an actual phone conversation. Do not feel special because a guy has texted you late into the night. Not only does he not want to pick up the phone and call you, but he may be holding "textversations" with other women simultaneously.

Suggestions to reduce the texting

1. Pick up the phone and call him. Sometimes all it takes is someone to get the ball rolling.

2. If he says he's at work, tell him to just call on his break. Everybody gets some type of break, lunch, and sometimes both, unless they only work a few hours daily. In that case, he has time to call you after work.

3. Pay attention to if he calls you before/after work. Many guys have reported that they like to hear from a woman they're interested in when they wake up, or after they've had a long day and want to wind down.

4. Never be afraid to say "Call me". If he's already texting you, this should be no problem. If it is, then that's definitely a red flag.

He's not looking for anything serious

How many times have you heard this magical line? This line is the anthem for Mr. No Good, from the Ladies' Man all the way to the Taken but Looking guy. Anytime a guy tells you this, it's best to just keep walking, because they mean it. There's no amount of taming or charming you can do to change his mind. He won't change until he's ready to. In the world of dating, there aren't too many reasons for not wanting anything serious.

- He wants to be able to date who he wants, and however many he wants.
- He's already in a serious relationship of some sort, and is looking for someone to have on the side.
- He's married and looking.
- He lives with his partner, and can't take you home, or too many public places.

It all boils down to the fact that he does not want to be tied down to you, and doesn't want you nagging him about doing so. This is why he tells you up front. I applaud men that say this in the beginning. You should be happy that they aren't playing mind games with you, no matter what the reason is that they don't want anything serious. Letting you know they're not looking for something serious keeps you from wasting time. Any decision made to keep dealing with that guy from that point on, or developing feelings for him, is completely on you. However, be real with yourself. Keep in mind the possibility of feelings developing, and the fact that there will be other women in his life. Ask yourself if this is something you want to deal with.

He lies, even about simple things

This should be pretty self explanatory. Any man that lies to you is no good for you. Lies always mean there is something to hide. It also means that they don't respect you enough to tell you the truth. If you're anything like me, lies are the ultimate pet peeve. I feel that when a person lies to you, they are insulting your intelligence, and for no good reason at all.

The Ladies' Man wouldn't be as horrible to tolerate minus the dishonesty. There are some men out there that will tell you they have other women they are seeing and/or sleeping with, and they leave the decision on you as to whether you want to continue. This may not be what you want to hear, but at least it is honesty.

But the fact remains the same….most ladies' men lie. In their eyes, they lie for good reason. They lie to protect your feelings and to "keep the peace". Most feel that they're so used to doing it, that they will never be caught.

<u>Examples of common lies</u>

"I'm at work, text me"

"I was asleep last night when you called"

"I'm hanging out with my boys"

"I have my son/daughter tonight"

"I have other friends, but I'm only sleeping with you"

"She's like a sister"

"I want to be with you, I just need to get my finances/life together first"

"My phone went/is going dead"

"I don't know why she's looking at you like that, we're just cool"

"I don't like to talk on the phone"

Simple lies have always been interesting to me. Some of the lies the Ladies' Man tells can be so unnecessary. I used to just laugh little lies off and think "What was the point of that?", but what I've learned over the years is that those little lies should be paid attention to. **If a man can lie to you about something simple and of no consequence, they will definitely lie to you over something more serious that will bring them an undesired consequence.**

The simple lies also say a lot about his character. Telling random lies brings out his dishonesty, as well as his capability of manipulation. What else and who else could he be lying about? Who else is he lying to? These "little" lies also need to be paid attention to, because most of the time they lead to an even bigger lie. The lie told about him getting off work at 5pm instead of 3pm could be the cover up for him going to take one of his other women on a lunch date, while he tells you he works overtime. Make sure you're not sweeping lies under the rug. Attention to detail in dating and relationships is just as important as it is in your line of work.

He over explains things

This trait of Mr. Ladies' Man goes well with the lying section. Have you ever dated a guy that had an extremely detailed story for any time he didn't answer your call, or didn't follow through with plans to spend time with you? Something crazy, but seemingly realistic always seems to happen to him on the day that you're supposed to hang out, doesn't it? More than likely he's not as accident prone or bad luck bound as he is making himself out to be. He's just good at making up lies. This doesn't mean go around accusing any and every guy that has unfortunate incidents occur of lying. Be reasonable. People do have unfortunate circumstances arise, but be smart. If this is going on often, it may be excuses.

Take Pat, for instance. Pat had a lot going on while we were dating. He worked 2 jobs, was working to open his own business, and he would have his son on Tuesdays, Thursdays, and every other weekend. Pat was extremely charming, but was definitely a ladies' man. He would call a lot and I would see him enough weekly that I was pleased with the way things were going. Then I started to notice a pattern in when we saw each other, as well as in his no call no shows. Pat would go missing for a day, sometimes even when we had made plans to spend time. Then he would wake up and call on his way to work, apologizing and telling me how his son's mother got sick and asked can he watch him. Other lies he used regarded his father's blood sugar level, and having to stay over there to monitor him, his sister getting into fender benders, his second job calling him in to work, or just that he laid down for a nap and slept for the rest of the night.

These were all definitely believable reasons. However, once I began to pay attention, I realized that these circumstances always fell on the weekends he didn't have his son, or it was days that a major game was coming on. It finally dawned on me, after catching him changing up his excuses without realizing it, that he was seeing someone else on those weekends, as well as setting me aside to host game nights with his friends and his ex wife.

He has a lot of women in his life

This problem can be very controversial. Sometimes it's hard to tell if a guy is involved with any of his female friends. Some guys have many female acquaintances from school, or they tend to hang out with their female family members. They may just have a lot of women in their lives, and they're not intimate with them. This can be really tricky.

Examples of men with a lot of females in their life

A man with "play sisters"

A man with baby mamas

A man still cool with his exes

A man that has "friends" he chills with, no strings attached

Men that work in female dominated workplace (gyms, hospitals, etc)

Situations like these can be problematic because it's hard to know for sure if they've been intimate with the females they're surrounded by. In college, many of the guys on campus would call certain females their "sister", when in fact it was someone they were sleeping with or had slept with in the past. It was their way of still being able to remain around those women while they were in relationships.

The baby mama scenario is very clear. The two have obviously been intimate at some point to make a child. This is usually a special bond, and there is a lot of truth in the statement that a guy is usually able to remain intimate with their child's mother whenever it's convenient. It is not true for every situation, but don't sleep on the possibility of it. Having had that situation myself, I can say that it's hard not to be intimate when two still have strong feelings for each other.

Be real with yourself: If your guy is still living with his child's mother, please be smart. If they are still living together, they are involved to some capacity. They may not have a title, but are very much intimate. Otherwise, they would not be living together. Don't believe the excuse that he's just "helping her get on her feet". There's more than that going on in the home.

The case of the ex

There will always be an ongoing debate about whether

exes can truly be friends. With so many things to consider and be careful of, it may be best to steer clear of a man that is still hanging out heavily with his ex, especially if you have trust issues. Most of the time at least one of them still has feelings, and is hanging on by using friendship as a crutch. Unless you are all hanging out together, you will most likely not be comfortable about their relationship, whether you admit it or not. This is especially true if the guy is not exclusive with you. Instead of cross examining how she became a girlfriend, and wondering if they sill mess around, leave this situation where it's at.

Substitution of things for time

The ladies' man, if he has the means for it, will sometimes shower you with gifts, and financial assistance in the place of spending a lot of time with you. If you've ever dated a professional athlete or someone in a high profile profession, you've more than likely experienced this. I'm not saying that most of them behave in this manner, but a lot of them do. They don't have a lot of time, and may not even live in the same city or state as you, so they buy you things and see you when they can, or when it's convenient for them.

Athletes are just one example of the ladies' men that substitute money for time. Any guy that is making decent money, whether it is from working multiple jobs to selling drugs, can have the tendency to fall into this category. Mr. Ladies' Man will pay for a few meals and bills here and there, but never really be around when you want to spend quality time. So many women brag about their "boos" that pay phone bills, pay for them and their girls to go out, and buy them outfits. These things are nice, and may make you happy, but how long will they be able to satisfy you in place of a good companion?

NOTES

_____

_____

_____

_____

_____

_____

_____

_____

_____

_____

_____

_____

_____

_____

_____

_____

_____

Chapter 2-Mr. Mentally Abusive

Mr. Mentally Abusive is a very common no good man. However, he seems to be the one that is least detected. This guy will mentally break you down, and feel no remorse about it. Usually women that are married, in long term relationships, and these with children for an ex or current boyfriend are more likely to encounter this guy. However, there are some cases of short relationships and "the other woman" situations that experience this type of behavior displayed by a mentally abusive man.

A man is most likely mentally abusive if he engages in any of the following behaviors:

- He tries to control you
- He says embarrassing things about you in public
- He's unsupportive of your goals, plans, and aspirations
- He isn't there for you when you need emotional support
- He ignores your feelings and concerns
- He says rude and degrading things about you
- He tells you no one else will want you
- He criticizes things you say often

Does your guy engage in any of the behaviors listed? If so, you're definitely dealing with Mr. No Good, and it's time to do something about it!

He tries to control you

When a guy tries to control most of the relationship, as well as your own life choices, he is showing that he finds you incapable of making good, responsible decisions. He is trying to take the reins on your life, which can be mentally exhausting for you to deal with. This is especially evident in instances, like the following:

- He makes you dress a certain way
- He tells you who you can and can't hang out with
- He controls your financial transactions, and keeps your money, rationing it as he sees fit
- He keeps you from spending time with family
- He only lets you call or text him at certain times

The controlling is a way for Mr. Mentally Abusive to ensure that you have no outside influence on how things should be. This behavior is actually a form of masking all his insecurities. There is no such thing as controlling someone else in a healthy relationship. You should have a mind of your own, and be able to make decisions on your own life. You should also have a voice in your situation with your partner.

DID YOU KNOW: Controlling is a form of domestic abuse.

Don't get caught up in making excuses for controlling behavior. Common excuses include:

- "I like when a man takes charge"
- "He likes when I dress this way and I don't mind dressing to please him"
- "Those friends are no good for me anyway"
- I'm bad with my money, so I don't mind if he keeps it"
- "I do tend to spend too much time with my family"

He says rude and degrading things about you

Mr. Mentally Abusive can be pinpointed the easiest with this characteristic trait. Any man that will deliberately say hurtful, degrading things about you, whether when you two are alone or in the company of others, is trying to make you feel and look inferior. He knows that saying these kinds of things will make you begin to doubt yourself. Sometimes, it can make you think twice when someone you feel cares about you, tells you something hurtful. Depending on how bad, or close to truth it may be, it's not always that easy to just assume that he's saying things because he's angry. What if he's not angry at all?

It's important to get out of a situation with someone that says horrible things to you as soon as possible. It's not your best interest he holds at heart. He wants to make you feel interior, so that he can control your emotions and self image. When making excuses for why you are putting up with this nonsense, you are continuing to put life-and how you view yourself- in his control.

Things Mr. Mentally Abusive will say

- You're fat/skinny
- You're ugly
- You're a whore
- Nobody wants you
- You're a setback for me
- No one likes you
- You're worthless
- You're a loser
- You make me sick
- No one loves you
- You're good for nothing
- I don't like you, I tolerate you
- You're dumb
- You're a crybaby
- Your/my family hates you

You may be sitting here right now making major excuses when going over the list above. It's hard to face the reality of the hurt in those words. Let's go ahead and cover the excuses I'm sure you might be thinking, or have made in the past while talking to others.

"He's just playing." This is one of the most common, yet most absurd excuses I've heard. How can someone say something so hurtful and embarrassing, but just be joking? Is bashing someone that he's dating his idea of a joke? It's not a funny one.

Is he really joking? I've always been told that a joke is 90% humor, but 10% truth, and over time I've learned that the percentage is more like 80/20, or even 60/40, depending on who it's coming from. Any man that will say something hurtful or mean to you as a joke is being abusive. He knows that saying those things will hurt you, and make you start showing concern about the topic addressed. With some of the men I spoke to while doing research for this book, I learned that men will often crack jokes about things that they don't like about their partner, in hopes that she'll get the hint and change it. Some said that they felt that their partner wouldn't handle the truth well if it wasn't in the form of a joke. Others stated that it lightened up breaking the truth to their partner. All the explanations I received all centered on the fact that there was major truths in their joking. Don't be so quick to laugh off a joke your guy makes about your appearance or something you're sensitive about. This only encourages the mentally abusive behavior. It's not just fun and games if it hurts someone. It's only fun for him, and it shouldn't be.

Are you only trying to convince yourself and others that he's "just playing"? Most likely, you know that he's not joking around. You may have thrown that in there in an attempt to save face, because when you told your girls about it, they told you he's trifling. Don't act like you haven't had the conversation before, where you were telling your girlfriend about one of you and your guy's episodes, and she started telling you that you need to leave him alone, or gave that disapproving silence you know all too well. In that instance, you immediately start giving excuses as to why it's not that big of a deal or trying to downplay the situation, because you don't really want to feel embarrassed or judged.

Another scenario is when your guy says something rude or degrading about you in front of others. Since there's no escaping what was said, the only thing you felt that you could do was later tell them he was just joking, or blame it on alcohol. Dodging his embarrassment is mentally exhausting in itself, and then you have to work to come up with ways to cover it up, or downplay it. Is it really worth it, just to have someone by your side?

"He's just angry." This is a common excuse used by not only the victim, but the no good man that actually makes the comments. We tend to say a lot of things we don't mean when we're upset. However, that doesn't make it right. Anger is a very dangerous emotion, and most mentally abusive guys will take advantage of this opportunity to say all the things they've wanted to say all along. Mentally abusive guys don't know or understand the concept of "fighting fair" because they've aimed to hurt and degrade for the longest. Pay attention to when he gets angry. Is it provoked? If not, more than likely it's anger that comes from within, and he feels better taking it out on you. It's best to remove yourself from the area if he's upset, to avoid getting your feelings hurt.

"I started it." This excuse is one of the worst because you are blaming yourself, which is what Mr. Mentally Abusive wants you to do. It's just another form of control. You may have said things that he didn't like in the middle of the argument, but that is never an excuse to degrade someone. As adults, we should learn to get our point across without insulting or "hitting below the belt". We shouldn't get caught in tit for tat behavior and retaliation either, especially in relationships. Most women show weakness when dealing with Mr. Mentally Abusive, and often take the blame, when they've done nothing wrong. They find a reason to satisfy making their partner upset, in hopes of gaining an understanding as to why they get treated the way they do. Often, they blame themselves and apologize just to stop the criticism and hurtful things that are being said. No more blaming yourself for Mr. Mentally Abusive's deeper rooted problems.

"It's true, how can I get mad?" It's time for a little bit of tough love. This is one of the worst things you could ever say when getting treated like less than a human being. You have a right to be upset whenever anything is said to insult or degrade you. Just because you've gained a few pounds doesn't give anyone the right to call you a fat slob. Just because you have a promiscuous past doesn't make it okay for him to call you a whore or slut. Agreeing with insults directed towards you is showing you have no self respect. How can you expect someone to respect you, if you don't even respect yourself? No matter how true something is, there's always a right and wrong way to say it. The truth hurts at times, but it's important to understand the difference between something being said to help you, and something being said to hurt or embarrass you.

Helpful words

- "We should start working out."
- "There are things about your past that bother me."
- "Want to help me clean up the house?"
- "I don't think that's the right answer."
- "We should go get checkups together."
- "Why don't you try a new look to switch things up?

Hurtful words

- "You're getting fat."
- "You're a hoe."
- "You're lazy."
- "You're dumb."
- "You smell bad."
- "You're unattractive."

He's unsupportive

This is a trait of Mr. Mentally Abusive that goes

undetected the most. People ignore the unsupportive nature of their partner unless it's extreme. Anytime your partner ignores or avoids talk about your plans for yourself or what you want out of the relationship, he is being unsupportive. He is showing you that your plans and thoughts are unimportant to him, and that he could be doing something better with his time.

Another example of being unsupportive is the obvious negative statements, such as "you can't do that", "you're not smart/pretty/slim enough", and "you'll never make it that far". These comments may be coming from true feelings, however they're obviously meant to hurt and discourage you from reaching your goal.

What good is having an unsupportive partner? If he doesn't believe in your potential, then why in the world is he with you? A partner is supposed to be encouraging and lift you up, not tear your goals and dreams down. Make no mistake; there is a huge difference in being realistic and being discouraging. Mr. Mentally Abusive tries to disable you from achieving goals and doing what you want to do with your life because it takes away from his control and power he currently has over you. He also doesn't want you to do better in life than him, because he feels superior due to the power you've given him up to this point. He knows that saying discouraging things will make you begin to believe him, and doubt yourself, which in turn will lead you to deciding not to keep moving forward.

He shows no concern when you need emotional support

Mr. Mentally Abusive isn't compassionate toward his partner as he should be. When unfortunate incidents occur, such as loss of job, death of family member or friend, and other serious events, he doesn't take the time to be there for you. Instead, he leaves you to deal with all the emotions you may feel in the best way you can. Often, he'll make comments, such as:

- "Quit being a crybaby. It's not that serious."
- "Go talk to your friends about it."
- "You need to get a journal or something."
- "I don't have time to throw you a pity party."

It doesn't take a husband or long term partner to give emotional support to someone. Of course you don't want to unload all your woes onto someone you've just met, but most have the ability to be compassionate. Sometimes all it takes is encouraging words, prayer, and a listening ear. In a relationship, these things should be a requirement. If your partner can't pray for you, listen to you, and try to help you feel better, how can they care enough about you to treat you right?

Warning: The kind of emotional support I speak does not mean going to your partner anytime the actor in your favorite show or movie dies, or anytime you and your friends disagree about something. Most men don't want to be treated like another one of your girlfriends. Be careful to not take advantage of getting emotional support over petty things. That could easily burn anyone out.

He tells you no one else will want you

Many mentally abusive guys say this at one time or another to their partner in an attempt to brainwash her to think there is no point in going look elsewhere. This statement is used to make his partner feel they have nothing to offer anyone else. Most of the time Mr. Mentally Abusive will add reasons, like:

- "You're fat."
- "You're too old to date again."
- "You're not good in bed."
- "You have a kid"/"You have too many kids."
- "You're too unattractive."
- "You're boring and have nothing to offer anyone."
- "You're broke."

Statements like this shouldn't get you down and out, because if you really were such a horrible option, he wouldn't be trying so hard to keep you around by scaring away the thought of moving on. Also, he wouldn't be with you himself if he thought you were that bad off. However, you should take into account that he doesn't respect you enough not to say horrible things to you and about you. If he was more respectful of you, he would express his feelings in a more mature and nicer way.

CHECKLIST

1. Does he often say hurtful things to you?

2. Does he say embarrassing or degrading things about you or to you, in front of others?
3. Does he cuss at you often?
4. Is he indifferent to your concerns and feelings?
5. Does he appear remorseful when he makes you cry?
6. Is he emotionally there for you when unfortunate things happen?
7. Does he have more negative things to say about you than positive things?
8. Do you feel unsupported in your goals and dreams?

NOTES

_____
_____
_____
_____
_____
_____
_____
_____
_____
_____

Chapter 3-Mr. Physically Abusive

Mr. Physically Abusive is the most dangerous type of no good man you can ever encounter. He is full of anger, and doesn't mind taking it out on others. In fact, he usually enjoys taking it out on others. Instead of using words to express himself, he would rather put his hands on you. **Physical abuse is never okay.** If a man cannot keep his hands to himself, he should not endanger anyone else by getting into a relationship until this behavior is nonexistent.

Often, Mr. Physically Abusive targets seemingly weaker, more submissive women to be in relationships with. Once he sees that he can talk to you any kind of way, he takes it a step further in controlling you by instilling the fear of being hit or beat up. He also is more likely to be abusive to the mother of his kid (if he has any), or younger women. These three types of women make him feel as he's in control. He feeds on their weakness and fear of him.

There are many possible reasons for why Mr. Physically Abusive resorts to violence, although the behavior is never acceptable. Most have underlying anger management issues that have never been appropriately addressed and treated. Some have experienced physical abuse their whole childhood, or have experienced their mother or female family members being abused, and feel that's how things should be. They haven't yet broken the vicious cycle they were exposed to. **Mr. Physical Abusive**

cannot heal himself, he must get help.

Common Excuses Used

"He only hits me when he's angry/under the influence of drugs or alcohol."

"I hit him first."

"I deserve it."

"He's had a long day, and I didn't have the house clean as I should have."

"It only happened once."

"He won't hit me anymore now that we're engaged."

"He's in anger management, so he's done abusing me."

The excuses are never ending when dealing with Mr. Physically Abusive, especially if others have witnessed the abuse. **It is never okay for a man to abuse his partner, no matter what you have done, said, or forgotten to do.**

Abuse is never your fault. However, **the same way men should be taught not to put their hands on women, is the same way women should be taught not to put their hands on men.** There's no double standard. It's best to remove yourself from a situation before you resort to violence. That's also the easiest thing to do.

Characteristic Traits of Physically Abusive Guys

Controlling   Easily Angered

Mentally Abusive   Gets into fights/altercations often

Often jealous   Very aggressive

Indifferent to tears/pain   Very apologetic/unapologetic

Makes you withdraw from friends/family

Sexually aggressive   Drinks/does drugs often

He is controlling and mentally abusive.

Mr. Physically Abusive has many of the same characteristic traits as Mr. Mentally Abusive. They are more interested in controlling their partner rather than being in a mutual relationship, and enjoying it. In having control, he feels like more of a man, and that he has things in order in his life. The only difference is Mr. Physically Abusive uses physical force to gain and maintain his control, whereas the mental abuser uses the power of hurtful words.

In efforts to control you, Mr. Physically Abusive will make you decrease communication with friends and family. He doesn't want to risk everyone finding out how he treats you, and trying to talk into leaving him. He also doesn't want you enjoying too much time with others, or having too much of an opportunity to meet a new guy that may

41

treat you better.

He is easily angered.

Mr. Physically Abusive often gets angry, and at times, over the smallest things. He may see that laundry wasn't done, or that his meal wasn't cooked the way he likes. He may get upset at a comment or joke made in front of others, or the fact that you didn't answer the phone when he called. It's one thing to be upset or disappointed, but pay attention to if he begins yelling, slamming things around, or stays angry for long periods of time. Most likely, the problem is deeper than just you cooking fish instead of chicken.

He gets jealous often.

The physically abusive guy tends to have above average jealousy. He will get visibly upset if he even thinks you're flirting or checking out a guy. He will make you change clothes if he feels you may look too appealing to others. He often is ready for a fight or feels disrespected if other guys are paying too much attention to you. He views you as his property, and feels offended if anyone, including you, thinks otherwise.

He is sexually aggressive.

Some physical abusers are also very forceful sexually. He may force you to do things you don't feel comfortable doing, be physically abusive during sex, refuse to stop when he can obviously tell you're in pain, or use unwanted objects on you. He is once again getting enjoyment out of overpowering you. In this case, sexual gratification is a major aspect of him feeling better about himself, and that he is in complete control.

Sexual assault can also occur in these ways. Examples include:

Ripping clothing off

Hindering you from putting clothes on

Grabbing body parts in a sexual manner

Pinning you down on the bed

Using foreign objects sexually to penetrate you

These are examples that may sound absurd to some, but they occur in some abusive relationships. Abusive men don't accept "no" for an answer, and there aren't too many things off limits to them. Sexually aggressive attacks can be extremely dangerous and devastating, and should always be taken seriously, no matter how well you know the person, or how much you feel the person may care about you. If he cared, he would not do something that hurts you, emotionally or physically.

<u>He hurts your kids.</u>

This situation usually poses a great debate, depending on who is involved in the conversation. A physically abusive guy may abuse your kid or children, if they are in the same home. If they can things as far as they do with you, don't take it for granted that they may raise a hand or a weapon to your children.

When I first began interviewing women about the contents of this chapter, the topic of disciplining kids came into play. Some women felt as if it is okay for their partner to physically discipline their child, even if the child is not his. Others felt that only a child's mother or father should be able to whip their kid. The question, in my opinion, was not who was disciplining their kid, but how the child was being disciplined.

I won't tell you how to raise your children, because that isn't the topic of this book, nor is it my place. However, I will say this: Some parents draw a very thin line between whipping a kid and beating a kid. It's never okay to beat a child, ever. I'm not saying tap a child's butt or their hand, and send them on the way, because I do believe in a good butt whipping. However, letting someone completely abuse your child is unacceptable. It's important to be careful about dealing with a physically abusive guy, because if he will hurt you, he can and might hurt them. Having a relationship is not worth risking the wellbeing of your child. Your child risks being seriously injured or, even worse, killed. That would be a very hard pill to swallow. The same goes for a sexually abusive guy. I'm not saying that every abusive guy molests children, because they don't. It is just something to pay attention to, because children are being molested and victimized more and more often these days, and if you can help to avoid it happening in your own household, do so. Your child is a very invaluable part of your life. He or she should be enough to leave an abusive relationship, so as not to risk him/her of being hurt too, as well as to avoid them being indirectly taught that behavior is acceptable.

Here is a list of resources you can use to help you leave a physically abusive situation. Don't be afraid to get help. Forget about how you think it will make you look. Forget about what your family will think. Set aside the thought of how much you may love your partner, and love yourself enough to save your life.

RESOURCES

National Domestic Violence Hotline

1800-799-SAFE(7233)

www.thehotline.org

National Center on Domestic and Sexual Violence

www.ncdsv.org

Battered Women's Justice Project

www.bwjp.org

www.loveisnotabuse.com –Liz Claiborne's teen dating violence website

Hubbard House

www.hubbardhouse.org

Georgia Domestic Abuse Hotline

1800-33-HAVEN (42836)

www.gcadv.org

Florida Domestic Abuse Hotline

1800-500-1119

www.fcadv.org

Alabama Domestic Abuse Hotline

1800-650-6522

www.acadv.org

Alaska Network on Domestic Violence and Sexual Assault

www.andvsa.org

Arizona Coalition against Domestic Violence

1800-799-7233

www.azcadv.org

Arkansas Coalition against Domestic Violence

1800-799-SAFE (7233)

www.domesticpeace.com

LADA Domestic Violence Hotline (Los Angeles)

1800-978-3600

www.Da.co.la.ca.us

Connecticut Coalition against Domestic Violence

www.cfcadv.org

Colorado Coalition against Domestic Violence

www.ccadv.org

Delaware Domestic Violence

http://Dvcc.delaware.gov

Hawaii State Coalition against Domestic Violence

www.hscadv.org

Idaho Domestic Violence

1800-926-2588 or 2-1-1

www.Idvsa.org

Illinois Coalition against Domestic Violence

www.ilcadv.org

Indiana Coalition against Domestic Violence

1800-332-7385

www.icadvinc.org

Iowa Coalition against Domestic Violence

1800-942-0333

www.icadv.org

Kansas Coalition against Domestic Violence

1888-END-ABUSE (363-2287)

www.kcsdv.org

Kentucky Domestic Violence Association

(502) 759-4050

www.kdva.org

Louisiana Domestic Violence Hotline

1800-978-3600

www.lcadv.org

Maine Domestic Violence Hotline

1800-624-8404

www.dahmw.org

Maryland Abuse Hotline

301-739-8975

www.avhotline.org

Massachusetts Abuse Hotline

1800-787-3224

www.aardvarc.org

Michigan Crisis Hotline

1800-942-4357

Minnesota Abuse Hotline

612-827-1795

Mississippi Emergency Crisis Hotline

1800-649-1092

www.findcounseling.com

Missouri Coalition against Domestic Violence

www.mocadsv.org

Montana Abuse Hotline

406-586-4111

www.mcadsv.com

Nebraska Abuse Hotline

1800-652-1999

www.ndvsac.org

Nevada Hotline

702-646-4981

www.nnadv.org

New Hampshire Coalition against Domestic and Sexual
Violence

1866-644-3574

www.nhcadsv.org

New Jersey Abuse Hotline

201-944-9600

www.njcbw.org

New York Domestic Violence Hotline

1800-621-HOPE (4673)

www.nyscadv.org

New Mexico Abuse Hotline

1800-773-3645

www.cabq.gov

North Carolina Abuse Hotline

1800-662-7030

www.nccadv.org

North Dakota Abuse Hotline

1800-472-2911

www.ycwawings.org

Ohio Abuse Hotline

1800-934-9840

www.odvn.org

Oklahoma Domestic Violence Hotline

1800-656-4673

www.ocadvsa.org

Oregon Abuse Hotline

1888-235-5333

Pennsylvania Abuse Hotline

1800-692-7445

www.pcadv.org

Rhode Island Abuse Hotline

401-467-9940

www.ricadv.org

South Carolina Abuse Hotline

www.sccadvasa.org

South Dakota Abuse Hotline

1800-430-SAFE

www.sdnafvsa.com

Tennessee Abuse Hotline

1800-356-6767

www.tcadsv.org

Utah Abuse Hotline

801-444-9161

Vermont Abuse Hotline

1800-228-7395

www.vtnetwork.org

Virginia Abuse Hotline

1800-352-6513

www.vadv.org

Washington Abuse Hotline

1800-562-6025

www.wscadv.org

West Virginia Abuse Hotline

304-255-2559

www.wvdhhr.org

Wisconsin Abuse Hotline

1800-562-6025

www.wcadv.org

Wyoming Abuse Hotline

307-755-5481

Chapter 4- Mr. Drug Abuser

Mr. Drug Abuser is the next no good guy up to bat. He gets a high on life in a dangerous way. His way of dealing with life comes in the form of weed, coke, pill popping, crystal meth, prescription drugs, and other drugs that are used to make him feel good and forget his problems. Not only is he doing this illegally, it also turns him into a different person, and not always for the better.

When dealing with a drug abuser, it can be hard to break through to him emotionally, and the struggle to get him to open up is even more difficult. Drugs tend to take over, and affect people in ways that they usually don't notice. However, the situation can be highly stressful and devastating to those around him who are affected, directly as well as indirectly.

Characteristic Traits of Mr. Drug Abuser

Spends a lot of money supporting his habit

Doesn't take care of his responsibilities as he should

Needs his drug of choice to function daily

Tends to be more aggressive at times

Spends more time satisfying his habit than with you or kids

Indifferent to your concern about drug use

Doesn't think he has a drug problem

It's hard to generalize how drug abusers get their start, because most of the time, the reasons are different. There are some that tried drugs due to peer pressure, and got hooked. Some grew up seeing their parents doing drugs, and went on to allow it as a normal part of their own life. Some experienced difficult, traumatic times, and turned to drugs to help them cope. Drug use is definitely a major epidemic today, and the victims, whether hooked, crying out for help, or doing it for recreation- don't need judgment or ill treatment. What they need is help and prayer.

Many women make the mistake of staying in relationships with drug users, as an attempt to "save them from themselves". This is nothing more than an excuse to remain in a relationship, and remaining while someone is poisoning themselves is nothing but enabling at its finest. If you really want to help, you'd be finding the resources he needs instead of sitting around in silence as he slowly self destructs. You can help someone at a distance. Being in a relationship with a drug abuser isn't a safe place to be, because drugs put your mind in an altered state. You never know when you'll have to suffer at the hands of someone who's had a "bad trip" or suffered an imbalance that makes him flip out on any and everyone around him.

The problem is magnified even more when there are kids involved. A person under the influence of drugs is in no way a good candidate for supervising a child. Yet so many women will leave their child in the care of someone that gets high daily. Drugs and children should never mix. A child shouldn't have to see his parents doing drugs. This can be a contributing factor to whether they will later pick up the dangerous habit as well.

Weed

Marijuana…there will always be a debate about this topic. Some states have legalized weed, some have made legal forms of it. When you talk to people of all different backgrounds, some will say weed is not really a drug. The bottom line is that weed alters your state of mind just like any other drug. Therefore it should be treated as such. Often, women don't take guys that smoke weed as any kind of serious threat, most likely because many of them get high too, or used to. I say this: If the Department of Children and Families can come and take your child away because of it, then it shouldn't be done. Weed is just as damaging to your body as any other drug on the market if used in excess, even if it "of the earth".

He spends a lot of money on his habit.

Drugs obviously aren't the cheapest, especially if the guy is a frequent user. Most drug abusers spend ridiculous amounts of money scoring the drug of their choice. Depending on which drug is their preference, some spend from hundreds to thousands monthly just to make sure their habit is satisfied. A drug user will often spend his last on his habit, or skip out on paying certain bills just to make sure they can get high. This is not the kind of man you need in your life. You will end up footing bills on your own, instead of your guy helping to provide for the household. There are many drug abusers that will even steal from their partners, or pawn all their things to get their fix. All of these can affect you financially and emotionally. It's not healthy to engage in a relationship with these things going on.

He doesn't handle his responsibilities.

Mr. Drug Abuser will skip out on handling responsibilities, minor and major. His altered mind state may make him forget things, like paying the water bill, signing your kid's homework, mowing the lawn, and medical appointments. He may forget about your lunch date, or special days, like your anniversary or a friend's wedding. Not only is he forgetful of things, he also will not feel up to doing things he should do. Some drug abusers would rather just chill all day, "enjoy their high', and take naps. It's all in the effect the drug has on his body. This behavior can get very frustrating, because the responsibilities now lie completely on you. You have to go behind him to correct everything, or simply do everything he just didn't do. This takes away from the 50/50 relationship, and puts a lot of strain on you. It can be very difficult to handle your business and daily duties, while trying to handle all of his as well.

He needs drugs to function.

Many drug abusers feel that they need their drug of choice in order to function day to day. Some may not say it, but it shows as they use the drug daily, or anytime they're happy, sad, bored, mad, lonely, etc. This is a surefire way to see that your partner has an extreme dependence on the drug. Many will defend their use of drugs, especially weed, by saying it helps them to calm down or relax their nerves. Don't pay attention to what it does for them, pay attention to their dependence. They are basically saying they can't survive without it. They don't feel "normal" or "right" without that drug in their system. Have you experienced that in your relationship, where your guy was extra cranky until he got high? Every little thing bothered him. What kind of bond do you really feel you have with a man that has to get "lifted" in order to be around you? The happiness and chemistry two share in a relationship should be all the high he needs, not one he has to harm himself to get. This isn't just unhealthy for him, it's completely unfair to you.

<u>He tends to be more aggressive.</u>

Some drug abusers resort to violence or have an elevated amount of anger when they are under the influence. There are some that will get into fights at the drop of a dime, because in their altered state, they feel others are looking at them wrong or "trying them".

Here's an example. One night, one of my guy friends was walking me to my car after leaving a nightclub. He was standing outside my car, saying good night, and there were three guys nearby standing outside of another vehicle. One guy was yelling and cursing at the other two, and they were trying to calm him down. He punched one guy in the face, and then began walking toward my friend, saying "I heard what you said!" My friend had no idea what he was talking about, but the guy decided to swing at him anyway, luckily falling to the ground in a failed attempt. His friend then held him on the ground until my friend walked away. The friend holding him down then explained to me that he had taken ecstasy and was just "tripping". He stated his friend does this often, and won't even remember it tomorrow.

Sad, but this is true of many drug users. They are likely to hear and see things that aren't there, depending on the drug. Many drugs bring on feelings of paranoia, anger, and hallucinations. They can also bring on sexually aggressive behavior, and cause a guy to not be able to control his behavior. Some examples of this include forcing a woman to have sex, groping her, kissing on random people, and much more. Your body is not able to control what drugs do, and even though he may use that same drug over and over, it may give a different reaction than before. This poses as a great danger not just for the drug abuser, but for the people around him as well.

<u>He spends more time satisfying his habit than with you.</u>

Mr. Drug Abuser will more than likely spend more time finding, using, and enjoying his drug of choice than actually spending quality time with you. His priority is getting high, and then dealing with whatever the day throws at him. This goes hand in hand with the feeling that he needs to get high to function, or start his day. He will spend a lot of time smoking with friends who also engage in drug use, or doing drugs alone.

This behavior has caused many women to have the mentality of "If you can' beat them, join them", especially when it comes to weed. Many women smoke marijuana today. At one point in time, it was deemed extremely unattractive and unladylike, but now it is widely accepted as the norm. Part of the reason for this is because some women have gotten sick of their partner never being around, and began smoking in order to share a hobby with him. That way, their man will be with them more. They also feel that will keep their guy away from hanging with other women that smoke, helping to reduce the likelihood that they'll cheat. Don't fall into that trap. Engaging in drug use to keep a man shows a very low case of self esteem and major weakness. Don't be a part of the problem, be a part of the solution.

He's indifferent to your concern over his drug use.

If you are in a relationship with a drug abuser, more than likely you have experienced his stubbornness to quitting. Many drug abusers don't feel they have a problem or addiction. They feel they can quit when they want to. When someone tells them they should quit or slow down, they ignore the request because it's just not that serious to them. Some may get aggravated at the fact that someone's trying to tell them what to do with their body, and how to live their life. It can be very stressful and painful watching someone destroy themselves over time. It's hard to help someone who doesn't want to be helped.

Chapter 5-Mr. Cheater

Mr. Cheater is one of the most common forms of a no good man. He deceives by stepping out of his relationship to be with other women. He comes in many different ages, races, and sizes, and so do his other women. Mr. Cheater also comes in all income brackets. Don't think that because a man doesn't have a job or money that he is not capable of having multiple women.

Cheating has become more main stream over time, which is no surprise due to the sex-fueled society we live in. We are living in times where many are no longer satisfied with one partner, and sleeping around is no longer a bad thing to the majority. Having all the women, or all the men, seems to be the norm, whether you're single, or in a relationship.

The lack of loyalty doesn't discriminate on age. Many think men are more likely to cheat at younger ages, because they're still maturing and experiencing the world. However, older men do just as much cheating. It's not about your age, cheating is about challenge, conquering, and variety. There are some men I know well into their 40's that cheat more than the 20-somethings I know.

Mr. Cheater often feels bored with their partner at home, and wants something more challenging. They begin to feel that their relationship is falling into the same old routine. Some feel the need to step outside of their relationship, just to see if they have the same game they used to have. Then you have the majority of cheaters that just want something different every now and then. A guy once told me (when asked why he cheats on his girl when she's so good to him) "A guy may have t bone steak at home, but every now and then he still wants hamburger helper".

This brings me to my next point. When a guy is cheating, it is not because of anything you are doing wrong, or anything you're not doing. If you are doing your best to show him you care, and are happy to be with him, you have no reason to blame yourself. A cheater will cheat due to his selfish ways. It's his desire to have his cake and eat it too. Many will say that you must not be doing something right in the relationship, but that has absolutely nothing to do with a man that doesn't respect women. Mr. Cheater is set in his ways, and will step out even if you are the most beautiful, sweetest woman alive. It's not just you. There are women before you that he more than likely treated the same way. Don't go blaming yourself, because if he was decent man, he wouldn't cheat. A man with respect for women will say it's not working out and end things, before he goes off and lies with another woman behind her back, or he will tell you what's not working and try to come to a resolution to save the relationship.

Characteristics of Mr. Cheater

- Starts arguments for no reason
- Accuses you of cheating often
- Doesn't mind being away from you
- Blames you for his cheating ways
- Lies a lot
- Hangs out/works late a lot more than normal
- Will cheat over and over, if allowed
- Has no remorse/over exaggerates remorse when caught
- May flaunt his other women in public
- Usually has friends that cheat on their partners
- May have been raised by parents that cheated
- Doesn't want involvement when altercation between his women occur
- Has pass codes on everything
- Is on social networks excessively, especially at night
- Frequents the clubs/bars without you
- Would rather go places alone
- Tends to be defensive
- Maintains communication with past flings/exes
- Overly flirtatious
- Doesn't answer his phone during late hours
- Usually keeps phone on silent or face down while at home

He starts arguments

Ladies, this is one of the oldest tricks in the book. Mr. Cheater will start arguments with his partner, so that he can have a reason to storm out. This gives him a way to go spend time with his other woman, or give her a call. The argument is just something he can use as an excuse later. That way, he can say "I left to calm down/clear my head". Pay attention to these moments and what he does afterwards. Often, if he doesn't leave, he may go into the next room to use his phone or computer. He's more than likely not calling his friends or family to vent. Mr. Cheater needs a reason to say that you get on his nerve or make him unhappy. This, in his mind, justifies his stepping out of the relationship.

He accuses you of cheating

This is another way of telling that you have a Mr. No Good on your hands. Mr. Cheater will often accuse you of cheating, even if there is absolutely no reason to. This behavior is usually his attempt to take the focus off of his own cheating. By saying you're doing it, he thinks it will throw you into a mode of wondering what you can do to show him that you're loyal, and also backing off of his case about what he may be doing. This also can be a major sign of his paranoid conscience, because a cheater knows that if it's that easy for him to cheat, it can be that easy for his partner to do the same to him. So he takes any little thing he can find in order to feed his accusations of your infidelity.

Tip: Pay attention to how he behaves when he thinks you're cheating. If his reaction is one that shows he doesn't care much, it's most likely because he's doing his own thing as well, or planning to do so.

<u>He doesn't mind being away from you for long periods</u>

Mr. Cheater knows that he needs time and space to do his dirt, so he doesn't mind if he has to spend a long time away from you. This does not mean that anyone that lives long distance or travels a lot is cheating. He will often suggest that he needs space, in order to ensure that he gets time with his other woman, or women. When he's gone for long periods of time, he may not be as excited to see you when he returns, or to hear from you often while he's away. Other times, he may be overly affectionate because he knows he's done something wrong. If he spends a lot of time away from you, and it's not work related, or he's okay with living in a separate city/state(even though there's nothing keeping him from being closer to you), these are possible red flags that he may be dealing with someone else. This doesn't mean that anyone who doesn't have a lot of time to spend with you has someone else on the side. Be reasonable. Usually there are signs that Mr. Cheater may be carrying on with someone other than you. We often choose to ignore these signs so that we don't have to address them and make changes. Every situation is different.

He's a repeat offender

Mr. Cheater will continue to cheat over and over again if there are no major consequences. I don't mean crying and depriving him of sex for a week or so. Most cheaters are stuck in their ways, and unless they have a major consequence, such as losing their partner, most will not stop what they're doing. They will more than likely just change up their methods of cheating so they won't get caught again. You are not helping make your situation any better by staying with a cheating man. You are only helping him perfect his craft, and creating more problems for yourself.

The grocery store in the neighborhood where I grew up used to have a section where you can buy pounds of candy in different assortments. The wrapped candies were in a large open container, and there was also a box that you drop 5 cents in to get one piece in case you didn't want to get a bunch. We would always go and just get a piece of candy, because it was unsupervised. It got to the point where many people would do this anytime they walked into the store, because they knew no one would say anything. Why? It was because there was no consequence for our actions.

It's the same for Mr. Cheater. He will continue to do as he pleases because you keep allowing him to. In his mind, the question is "Why should I only have one when I can have them all, and still have her?"

He hangs out/works late often

Be leery of a man that is always hanging out with the guys, or always working late. More than likely, it's his cover up for meeting up with another woman. Don't get me wrong, a guy needs his guy time, but pay attention to the frequency. If he starts hanging out with his friends way more than he normally does, there is something going on. Most likely, Mr. Cheater's friends will cover for him too, so there's no need to call around trying to track him down. It's a waste of energy and added stress. All it takes is a simple call/text to tell his friend "Hey, if my girl calls, I'm at your house", and then he's on his way to do whatever he has planned to do.

The "working late" excuse is a very old excuse, yet still tricks many people. If a man is working late all the time, his income needs to show for it. If not, he may be having a workplace fling, or leaving work to go spend time with someone else. Also, pay attention to the kind of work industry he is in, and the requirements of his job. Sometimes the "working late" excuse doesn't add up. If he's a bank teller, he's not at work until 11pm. If he works a government office job, he's not working through the night. If he's not working full time, he's more than likely not going on business trips and conferences on weekends.

He has pass codes on everything

This is an obvious sign that your guy might be cheating. There is no reason anyone should have all kinds of pass codes on their phone and computer login while in a relationship, other than the fact that they have something they are hiding. Mr. Cheater has probably had situations before where his creeping was discovered through his phone, and is protecting that from happening again. In the times we live in, sexting and virtual affairs have become extremely popular. Many women are sending everything but sex through pictures and video mail, causing Mr. Cheater to have to be more careful about covering his tracks. Pass code protection shows a lack of trust. Not only does it show that he can't be trusted, but it also shows that he doesn't trust you not to go through his phone.

He's on social networks excessively

Everybody likes a little Twitter, Facebook, and Instagram. Social networks are great marketing tools, and they are also great for keeping up with family members, friends in other states/countries, and colleagues. However, social networks are also an extremely popular venue for hook ups, emotional affairs, and meeting new people. Many cheaters have taken to the web to prowl for partners, because it's easier, and a more undetectable way of communicating. Mr. Cheater could sit at home all day, yet still be involved with other women. He could be sitting in the very next room, chatting and making plans to meet up with a local female, while you're watching television. This is also a great way for Mr. Cheater to reunite with females from his past.

Many cheaters get discovered through social networks, although many others never get found out. Pay attention to how often your guy frequents social networking sites. If he's not promoting or marketing, it shouldn't be much. Also, pay attention to whether he allows you to have access to his page. Some guys will give their partners limited access, or deny friend requests from their partner altogether. There are many that won't even display their relationship status on social networks, which is a major red flag that they are using the network to talk to other women.

He has no remorse/exaggerated sense of remorse

Mr. Cheater will usually go one of two ways when he is caught cheating. He will either not care at all, or go to the extreme, trying to make you forgive him. Normally when Mr. Cheater gets discovered more than once, it gets to the point where he knows there will be no consequence for his behavior, so he doesn't waste time pleading for your forgiveness. He instead develops a "get over it" attitude, because he already knows that after you yell, cry, and threaten to leave, it will be the end of whatever he has to deal with. Mr. Cheater knows that if he can get away with it once or twice, he can keep getting away with it.

A cheater that hasn't gotten caught isn't really sure how you will react to his behavior the first time he is caught. He doesn't know if you will actually leave, or just fuss. He's more likely to beg for forgiveness, beg you not to leave him, and even go as far as to cry in remorse for what he's done, in order for him to appear sincere. Sometimes it is a genuine gesture, but often it's just an attempt to keep you. He knows he has to pull out the "please don't go" routine, so that you can think that he's really not the cheating type, and that it was just an accident. Many women fall for this. It seems that a man that will cry and get on his knees to beg for forgiveness can win over a woman's broken heart easily. This behavior causes some women to believe that he must've really not meant to do what he did, and that he deserves more chances. So many think that all the crying and apologies is an automatic sign that he truly cares and will actually go bragging about how emotional he got when he thought he was going to lose them. They don't realize that it's not about how hard he tried to make it up to them. It's about the situation that never should've occurred in the first place.

When conflict occurs

So you've caught your man in a few lies, and then females start to call and play games on your phone. You have a good idea of what's going on, but instead of going with your gut feeling, you ask him what's going on. You know he's going to say he doesn't know why these females are calling, but this just gives you more time to justify staying with him, because there hasn't been any "in your face" evidence. Mr. Cheater will not admit anything until he absolutely feels there's no other way around the situation, and sometimes even then he won't tell the truth.

For instance, let's say a woman messages you online, and tells you she's been sleeping with your man. You write her back for details, and she responds giving them to you. When your confront Mr. Cheater, he may tell you that you're childish, and full of drama for wasting time talking to this woman that's making accusations. He'll criticize you in order to make you feel bad and throw you off track. He might even suggest that you block the woman, and ignore her, because she just wants to break you two up.

Another sign that he's cheating is when he says he doesn't want to be in the middle of the drama when you try to set things straight with him and the female(s) in question. Mr. Cheater doesn't want his cover blown, so he wouldn't dare put himself in a situation where he has to see or speak with the two of you at the same time. He doesn't want to have to admit he's cheating, and he also doesn't want to drive the other woman away by making a decision that may hurt her. Instead, he just avoids conflict completely. This behavior is seen a lot on social networks. There have been so many guys who have deactivated their profiles, or made their girlfriends deactivate theirs in order to keep their wrongdoings from being uncovered.

He stays in the club

Everyone knows that the clubs and bars are major pick up spots. More than likely, if your man is there all the time, without you, he's probably doing a little bit of picking up as well, or at the least doing a few things you wouldn't approve of. There's no reason a man or woman should always be out clubbing when they have a partner at home. People use the excuse of club promotion, but everyone knows club promoter get a bunch of attention from women, because many of them have the power to help these women gain access to the club or events. Mr. Cheater may frequent the club because it's an easy way to pick up women. There's a large amount of women there, and many of them are single and looking. The smartest thing to do if your man likes to party is to party with him.

Another sign that your man may be a cheater is if he gets bothered that you show up to the same club or event he's at. You would think that a faithful man would be more than happy for his partner to be at the same establishment as him. Instead, he may get upset, because he might be up to no good, and can't carry on like he normally would because you're there. You may have messed up his plans to leave early with a woman he was flirting with before you got there. Be smart. A good man won't leave his woman at home all the time to go and party.

<u>He would rather go places alone</u>

Mr. Cheater will normally look for any and every opportunity to meet up and/or talk with their other women. Often, they have to leave home to do so. Mr. Cheater will normally run errands alone, telling you that he'll be right back, or just simply saying that you can't accompany him.

In one of my past relationships, my ex would always say he's going grab a bite to eat, or say he had to get something from the store. In the beginning, these were errands we would always run together, and call them our little field trips. Then he began saying that I didn't need to ride because he'd be right back, or that he was going to smoke on the way there (he knew I couldn't stand it). I later found out that he was using those opportunities to call other women he was carrying on with. Every time he'd leave the house, he'd use it as an opportunity to return calls of women who had called earlier, or sometimes even meet them around the corner for a few minutes to see them.

The same can go for trips. Pay attention to him wanting to go on business or leisure trips alone. More than likely, he won't be alone for too long. Someone else may be accompanying him, or he may be planning to find a fling when he gets there.

Tip: Don't think that because he calls you a lot while he's gone that he can't possibly be cheating. It doesn't take long to step out on someone while in a relationship, and cheating is not confined to a certain time of day. This isn't to scare you, it's just to help you be more logical about the situation. So many seem to think that because their man calls them all day that they can't possibly have any time to call or meet up with anyone else, but this isn't true. If a man wants to see or talk to a woman, they will make time to do so.

<u>His phone is usually on silent, or turned face down</u>

These are obvious signs that you're dealing with Mr. Cheater. If a man always has his phone on silent while he's at home with you, or during sleeping hours, it's because he knows there's a possibility someone might be calling. He doesn't want to have to deal with explaining, so he just keeps his phone silent to make you think no one calls.

Another sign is when he always places his phone face down. This is to make sure that you not only don't see lights flashing as the phone rings, but also that you don't accidentally see who is calling or texting his phone. Think about it: why else would someone put their phone face down, risking scratching their screen?

Tip: Be watchful of a guy who always keeps his phone hidden, or in his grasp. He's making sure you don't get a chance to go through it, and he may also be using it to communicate when you're not in the room.

Examples: a guy putting his phone in his shoes, or leaving it in his pocket when he comes over to spend the night

A guy keeping his phone in his lap while you're out at dinner, or on the table

A guy bringing his phone with him into the bathroom to take a shower

Remember: These characteristics aren't to make you think that all men cheat, because they don't. They're just to help you figure out if your man is doing so, so that you can get rid of him, and find one that will treat you better.

He's nowhere to be found during sleeping hours

This one can be used whether you live with your man, or live apart. Daytime hours can be questionable, because people have lives, and engage in things that may keep them busy. However, not being able to get in touch with your man during sleeping hours is unacceptable. Your man should be reasonably accessible at all times. That doesn't mean you should blow his phone up all night, checking on him. This simply means there should be no excuses of "my phone went dead", "I didn't have a signal", "I was knocked out", and things like that.

Tip: Get to know the little things about your man, so that you can know his patterns. Does he sleep light? Is he a heavy sleeper? Does he normally go to bed early? Is he a night owl? If he sleeps light, then you know that he can probably hear his phone ringing to pick it up. If you know he stays up late at night, there's really no excuse why he can't pick up his phone. Be leery of these "I'm going to go to bed early tonight" goodnight calls. They may be calls just to get you out of the way for the night so that he can entertain someone else.

<u>Notes</u>

_____

_____

_____

_____

_____

_____

_____

_____

_____

_____

Chapter 6- Mr. Unavailable

It's time to introduce Mr. Unavailable, the guy that's already off the market. He is taken, but still looking. He has the woman, and possibly children, yet he still wants to have a little fun on the side. He's not looking to replace his woman. He knows that he's going to keep her by his side, and he just wants some random side play.

Mr. Unavailable is normally looking to fill a void in his relationship or marriage. He needs some excitement and misses the option of having variety. He feels that the fire has gone out, and that he could use some added spice. Sometimes, there's nothing wrong in his relationship, and he just wants attention from other women. Either way, he feels that he can step out of the relationship, and doesn't really think about hurting his significant other in the process.

Mr. Unavailable will normally try to hook up with women that he thinks are drama free, and can keep their situation a secret. He doesn't want to risk dealing with someone that will contact his significant other as soon as things don't go her way. He will also look for women that are well put together and accomplished, because he feels women have too much going for themselves to risk their affair being discovered. The same goes for his preference in someone who's already in a relationship or marriage themselves. He feels they're in the same boat, and can work together at keeping their relationship a secret. Other women Mr. Unavailable targets are younger, sometimes college students, and women with kids. With each of these types of women, he feels that he can keep them pleased sexually, and sometimes financially.

Many women have fallen into the habit of "sharing" men in order to have financial assistance. This is especially true of women with kids, and women that focus on gaining relationships for financial gain. They don't mind having a piece of a man, and devaluing themselves as long as their bills are paid, and they have money for leisure activities. We as women need to get out of this mindset.

Characteristics of Mr. Unavailable

- Claims he's separated, or in the process of divorce
- Always blames unhappiness on his partner
- Has a history of cheating on partners
- May not be accessible on holidays
- Doesn't really like taking pictures with you
- Doesn't like going in public with you
- Can never really spend consistent time with you

He tells you he's separated or in the middle of a divorce

This will almost always be Mr. Unavailable's story. If he's married, he will say he's currently separated, or that they're in the process of divorcing. If he's in a committed relationship, he may say that they're on a "break", or that it's been over between them for a long time now. The best thing to do is to wait until there's proof he's divorced or single before getting involved with this guy. Dealing with a taken man is not only pointless, it can also be very dangerous. It can get you tangled in a messy web of drama, resulting in things as serious as injury or death.

There's really no way of proving that the separation Mr. Unavailable speaks of really exists, so he uses this to his advantage. He knows that a woman that is desperate enough or weak minded enough will take that explanation and run with it. She's hoping that she can get something out of it, and possibly even end up with the man in the end. Mr. Unavailable rarely leaves his wife or girlfriend for the other woman. Also, even if he did leave her, you risk being treated the same way as she was treated. **If he cheats with you, he will cheat on you**.

He tells you he's been unhappy for a long time

This is another statement that you should be aware of. **If Mr. Unavailable was as unhappy as he claims to be, he would leave.** There would be nothing to keep him there. When that's addressed, he'll come up with every reason in the world why he can't leave just yet. He may say it's for the kids, he's waiting and saving up enough money, his partner has a long term illness, or that his partner keeps saying she'll kill herself if he leaves (yes, that is used often). Don't fall for this spill. He's trying to gain pity. A lot of times Mr. Unavailable is going around saying he's unhappy, when his relationship with his partner is fine. He just wants a little variety, or to see if he still has what it takes to keep the attention of other women. The cheating usually has nothing at all to do with the wife or girlfriend not handling their business in the relationship.

He is not accessible on holidays

If you're dealing with Mr. Unavailable, you've probably experienced this, whether you want to believe it or not. He had to spend his holiday elsewhere with his girlfriend or wife, and might not have been able to sneak away to see you. This is something that you will have to get used to if you're going to settle for being the other woman. So many women get involved with a man that already has a partner, and they make excuses as to why they can't spend the holidays or other special days with him. Some will even begin to try and convince others (as well as themselves) that they don't really need to spend a holiday with their partner. Holidays spent alone when you have somewhat of a significant other can be painful, whether you admit it or not. How long are you willing to put up with playing backup to someone else before you decide that you deserve someone that wants you and only you?

You're always on borrowed time

Anytime that you spend with Mr. Unavailable is never really going to be enough. He will most likely have to be home eventually, and can't stay overnight with you. He will also be inconsistent with spending time with you, unless you two have a neutral place you frequent (work, gym, etc). Otherwise, things will begin looking suspicious to his significant other. At the end of the day, his priority lies with his wife or girlfriend, making you just a convenient option. He will have to go home when his partner needs him. He will have to decline your offers to spend time because he is at home with her, and that will bother you. He will have to make arrangements with you based around making sure home is taken care of first. Is this really what you want to build a relationship on?

He doesn't like taking pictures or going in public with you

Mr. Unavailable (if he even cares about getting caught by his partner) will most likely avoid taking pictures with the other woman, for fear of it being incriminating for him. He knows that this can backfire on him at any time that the other woman may get upset with him. Not only that, he risks being exposed due to the possible posting of the pictures on social networks. Also, he may not want to take you certain places for fear of his significant other seeing the two of you, or finding out about the two of you from someone she knows. So you end up being confined to certain areas, which most likely don't even include his home.

Think about it: Don't be too quick to be impressed by Mr. Unavailable putting you up in a hotel room. Hotel room stays are nice, but keep in mind prostitutes get taken to hotel rooms to do their work too. More than likely Mr. Unavailable doesn't want to spend money on a room, but he'd rather do that than take you to his home. Sometimes, it's because his woman is there. Sometimes it's because he just doesn't want you knowing where he lives, so you don't pop back up

uninvited. It's not really anything to brag or be proud of. Don't be impressed with a guy that can't take you home.

<u>You risk conflict with his significant other, or other women</u>

Drama, drama, and more drama… If you are dealing with a taken man, or have dealt with one in the past, you have probably experienced some type of confrontation. It may have been by his wife, girlfriend, or simply one of his other women he's dating. This is a very embarrassing and uncomfortable situation, because deep down you know you're wrong for what you're doing. You find yourself in one of two pitiful situations. You will either have to lie to cover for a man that won't even respect you enough to have you as his one and only, or you'll have to address the allegations vaguely, confirming that you disrespected yourself by dealing with a man you know is taken. Both of these options are devaluing to self worth, an embarrassing blow.

<u>FYI</u>

- A man not wearing a ring doesn't mean a thing
- If he's that miserable and down (with his partner), he wouldn't be sticking around
- Sharing a man is no good for your health, you're hurting others and degrading yourself
- He's not a good man if he doesn't value his wedding band

85

- He'll say he's unhappy with his wife, even if he's having the time of his life
- There's nothing cute about being the spice that drives a man away from his wife
- If he cheats with you, he will cheat on you

NOTES

_____

_____

_____

_____

_____

_____

_____

_____

_____

_____

_____

_____

_____

_____

_____

_____

_____

_____

_____

Chapter 7- Mr. Immature

Mr. Immature is known for his boyish, childish ways. Make no mistake, though. He isn't always a young guy. There are many young guys that are more mature than some older guys.

He may seem harmless in the beginning stages of getting to know someone and dating them. For some, Mr. Immature may even be a breath of fresh air, with their carefree ways, and playful approach to life. Most of them know how to have a good time, mainly because they never really stopped having a good time after high school and/or college. However, there is a time for playing, and then there's a time to make sure that business is handled. This is where Mr. Immature turns into a bad option for you. They don't know exactly when to take things seriously. The carefree attitude, that may have once been cute to you, is now ruining your relationship. If he doesn't take important things in his life seriously, then he won't be able to really take you seriously.

Mr. Immature often looks for women that seem to have it all together, because it helps to balance things out for them. They feel that they'll look like they have it made by dating someone that is doing well, giving them bragging rights amongst their friends. This kind of woman also acts in a motherly way, keeping (or attempting to) the guy in line. It isn't the most ideal situation. This kind of mate cannot step up and take leadership in the relationship as a man should. Things tend to fall apart easily. Mr. Immature is more of a follower, and not a leader.

Characteristics of Mr. Immature

- He still focuses on keeping his friends' approval
- He's more worried about popularity and what looks cool, rather than leadership
- He feels validated as a man through what kind of women he can brag about having
- He is disrespectful in his approach with women
- He would rather hang with his friends than his partner
- He may stay in the clubs
- He doesn't view marriage as significant

He is too worried about keeping his friends' approval

Mr. Immature, just like in middle school and high school, still does things to impress his friends. He only seems to feel validated when his buddies approve of what he's doing, and who he's dating. The image and reputation he keeps with them is more important than establishing himself in life as a stand up man. He may talk firmly and condescendingly to you in front of his boys, so they continue to think he completely runs the relationship. He might go out and get phone numbers to compete with his friends, even if he doesn't plan on using the numbers. He might even go as far as to break up with you, to show his buddies that he's not "soft" and can be without a partner. His friends, although he'll never admit it, are in total mind control over him, and he shows it by doing whatever will keep them laughing or admiring him. He feels he's the man as long as all his friends think so.

He's still hungry for popularity

The desire to be accepted doesn't just stop with his friends. Mr. Immature still thrives on his level of popularity. He wants to be accepted as one of the cool people by all that encounter him. He engages in a lot of attention-seeking behavior, like talking recklessly or revealing too much information on social networks, referring to himself as something of celebrity status, making sure all women know him or know of him, and going out of his way to make sure he's the "life of the party". He may also brag about his bedroom skills to anyone that will listen. Gaining and maintaining popularity makes him feel accomplished, even if he hasn't done anything else significant. He tends to feel that one of the main things people strive for, aside from money, is to be known. This delusion of grandeur Mr. Immature possesses sustains him. This type of behavior can be detrimental to a relationship because his desire for popularity tends to overpower his will to maintain effort in his relationship for the right reasons. You may end up feeling lonely, unappreciated, and frustrated with his constant "putting on" for his audience. This can cause burnout in any relationship, long or short term.

He doesn't have much respect for women

Mr. Immature can be disrespectful to women in

different ways. He tends to feel that he's not disrespectful because he shows respect to his sister, mother and other family members. However, the same treatment doesn't apply for those he dates. Mr. Immature may refer to women as "bitches", "hoes", "sluts", and other degrading words when speaking about them. Not only does he verbally degrade women, but he may also treat women as objects. Mr. Immature still feels validated by how many women he can sleep with. He will treat women as pieces of meat and then move on to the next. This behavior is acceptable to him. We as women need to stop accepting this behavior, regardless of it seeming like it's the norm.

He needs women to make him feel accomplished

This behavior ties in with Mr. Immature's desire to be accepted and respected by his friends. He needs a lot of attention from women to feel like he's the man. He needs to feel that he can say he has the best looking women on his arm, as well as the most. Mr. Immature will collect phone numbers and even sleep with countless numbers of women in order to feel important and accomplished. Often, Mr. Immature competes with his buddies on who can get the most women. This behavior isn't good for any relationship, because he may not take the relationship seriously. This behavior may also cause him to be unfaithful in his relationship. Being in a relationship doesn't make him look like the man amongst his friends.

He avoids work, doesn't have ambition

Mr. Immature doesn't really want to work. He wants

things to come to him easily, or find women to give him the things he wants and needs. He likes the idea of fast money, but does not want to work too hard to be successful. He lacks ambition, and is usually known to just talk about all the things he's going to do, but never do them. He looks for quick, easy ways to make money. Mr. Immature has more of a hustler mentality, rather than strong work ethic. A good example of this a guy that would rather live the street life, selling drugs to get fast money, rather than going to work at a legal establishment, making an honest paycheck. He would rather do wrong to get money to get by.

Mr. Immature may jump from job to job, if he even has a job at all. He usually makes excuses for why he had to quit or why he was fired. It is, of course, never his fault. The truth is, he'd rather be somewhere hanging out than at work, bored. Of course, many people don't like to get up and go to work every day, but the difference is that most people understand the importance of stability, and get up and go to work because of that.

This behavior of avoiding work isn't good for relationships because it shows that he's not even willing to do what he needs to do in order to take care of himself, so it's highly unlikely that he will be able to do for you in your time of need. Not only that, he is showing that he is not a financially responsible person, and that can be important when making decisions regarding settling down with someone. You don't want someone that will break the bank, and leave you unable to pay your bills.

This hustler mentality Mr. Immature has can also be dangerous and stressful. If he is selling drugs, he risks being put in jail, being robbed, and he also puts himself, as well as you, in danger of possibly injury or even worse, death. Be careful who you allow into your life. You never know who they may be being targeted by, especially when they're in the drug dealing business.

He would rather hang out with his boys

Mr. Immature values his guy time, just like most, but he chooses it over spending time with his partner sometimes. This is very similar to boys' behavior in grade school. He may leave work and go unwind with his friends. He may wake up and go spend time with them, before his day gets fully started. This behavior can also be a red flag that he's seeing someone else, too. There's no way to properly build a successful relationship when both partners aren't fully involved and present most of the time. There's no need to argue this behavior with Mr. Immature either, because he will only say that you're trying to control him. He will convince himself that you're just trying to run his life, with possible added cosigning from his friends, because he lets them know everything that goes on in your relationship.

He stays in the clubs

Mr. Immature holds partying up high on his priority list. The club is his place of significance. He feels that he's the man there. There's plenty of women to flirt with and choose from, his boys are there, and plenty of people to show off for. The vibe he gets from the club environment makes him feel extremely popular, especially if a lot of people there recognize and show him love. He frequents the club to indulge in everything that he identifies with, everything that he feels makes him "the man". The behavior is similar to being in grade school, and wanting to attend every party to feel like he's a part of the "in crowd". He may use the excuse that he's young, or young at heart, as the reason he goes out every night. He also feels that it's okay as long as he has no major responsibilities.

He doesn't view marriage as a priority

Consider yourself "lucky" (and I use that term loosely) if you can get Mr. Immature into a relationship. He doesn't like to be in relationships, because he doesn't really want to be tied down. He tends to look at being in a committed relationship as something negative, like a burden. His mentality is to have all the women, instead of just one that won't give him everything he wants in a partner. Mr. Immature feels that he may not find one woman that provides everything he wants in a woman. Instead, he prefers to stick to his player ways. Marriage is something he views as a punishment, or something that takes his freedom away. Mr. Immature thinks of it as a miserable experience he doesn't want to have any time soon. This thinking is usually based on what they've seen or heard others say.

Chapter 8- Mr. Booty Call

We've all encountered this guy in the course of our lifetime, probably more than once or twice. This guy is looking for sex, plain and simple. He wants nothing more and nothing less. Mr. Booty Call will do and say whatever he can to get sex, even if it means deceiving you. He usually comes in disguise, although there are some of them that will bluntly tell you what they want from you. When he tells you he doesn't want anything serious, believe him. Don't hurt your own feelings trying to force something that your partner doesn't want. There's no need wasting time pretending to be okay with a "no strings attached" when you want something more, and there's no point in trying to change his mind to wanting a relationship. You will more than likely be unsuccessful in your attempts. He has made it clear what he wants. He also knows there are plenty of women willing to settle for the casual sex relationship he's looking for.

Most guys looking for casual sex will tell you that they're not looking for anything serious (he is similar to Mr. Ladies' Man in many ways) This is his way of telling you the truth without really having to be blunt, because he knows that there's a major possibility you won't be down with just being a booty call for him. He knows he may have to put in a little time and work in order to get what he wants. Some will even pretend that they're open to a relationship with you, because they know that it will give you hope that it can turn into something more.

94

Usually if Mr. Booty Call's motives don't show in the beginning in an obvious manner, they will eventually rise to the surface in a short period of time. Mr. Booty Call isn't going to continue showing a lot of interest if he sees he's not going to be able to get you in bed.

Characteristics of Mr. Booty Call

- Usually only calls/texts for arrangements to have sex
- Makes excuses about why he doesn't have time to hang out
- Tells you things to make you smile, but his actions don't line up with his words
- Keeps a rotation of women
- He's not looking for a relationship or anything serious
- May not want to go in public places with you
- Only spends time with you when sex is in the plan
- Decreases interest in you once he has sex with you

He calls/texts primarily for sex

Mr. Booty Call is after sex, and if you pay attention, it's usually pretty obvious. The main sign is his calling and texting during late hours. Usually Mr. Booty Call is calling at this time in hopes that the two of you can hook up and have sex without spending all the extra time. The plan is to catch you late at night, so that you're already in bed, or

95

have plans to get in bed soon, so that he can join you.

Many women today don't accept the late night communication for what it really is. Most make excuses for why they allow men to contact in these late night hours. It may come as a shock to some, but it used to be deemed disrespectful for a man to contact a woman too late in the evening. This is a standard that women should stick with in their process of changing their dating patterns (this will be discussed later). Most guys are calling during these hours because they want sex, or they have failed to make adequate time for you during the day or evening. Both of these are unacceptable reasons.

Mr. Booty Call will usually be calling/texting to find out if you're able to meet up, or have company. He doesn't call daily to inquire about your day, or just to hear your voice, not unless he knows this is what you require. His phone communication is used mainly to plan. He may make a little small talk here and there, but there will always be some kind of invitation, directly or indirectly, to have sex. Pay attention to the frequency of his calls. Is he calling just to chat and/or say hi? Is he calling to say that you're on his mind? He should. If he only wants sex, you're being used, whether you'd like to call it that or not.

He makes excuses for his lack of time

Mr. Booty Call is not trying to spend a lot of time chatting or hanging out with you, unless sex is involved. When pressed for why he never seems to have time, he will come up with a bunch of excuses why he's so busy. He may say he's always working, he's always with others and can't talk on the phone, he's with his kid, etc. It's funny that he always has time when he wants to have sex, but is so busy any other time.

Don't settle for this treatment. You need to demand more respect for yourself. Someone who only feels you're good enough to hang out with when you're giving it up shouldn't be worth any of your time. He is clearly showing you that he only values you sexually. A man that is too busy for you doesn't deserve to share a bed with you. Because Mr. Booty Call doesn't want to be stuck spending time with you or chatting you up to get what he wants, he may tell you up front that he is a busy guy, so that you won't expect much time with him. He is similar to Mr. Ladies' Man in many different ways.

His actions don't line up with his sweet nothings

When it comes to telling you what you want to hear, Mr. Booty Call is one of the best. He will shower you with compliments, and may even tell you how much he likes you, in order to make you feel special and appreciated. This isn't his first rodeo. He knows that women love this kind of treatment. This behavior is the strongest in the beginning, before he actually sleeps with you. Getting a woman in the bed is normally the hardest the first time around, so he lays on the sweetness and charm. However, if you pay attention, you will notice that a lot of the things he says to you don't match up with how he treats you. He may be barely calling, and barely spending time with you. He may not take you on

97

any dates. Actions will always speak louder than words, in any situation. Keeping this in mind while dating will never fail you when you're unsure whether to continue in your situations. **A guy that is truly into you will show it clearly, without any prompting.**

He usually has a rotation of women

Just like Mr. Ladies' Man, Mr. Booty Call may have more than one woman at a time. His objective is sex, and lots of it. He needs to make sure that he has someone that he can call at anytime he wants it. He knows that he risks one woman not always being on call for sex, so he knows his chances to get sex whenever he wants increase with the increase of women. Not only that, he can great variety with an assortment of women on standby, which will keep him from getting bored with the same partner. Having different women keeps his ego and sex drive satisfied, and he's very familiar with replacing, not chasing. Be careful not to settle for being a part of any guy's rotation.

He doesn't want a relationship or anything serious

This should come as no surprise. Mr. Booty Call knows that he doesn't have to be in a relationship to get relationship perks, or the sex he wants from a woman, so he avoids putting himself in that position. He may say that he's just going to let things flow and see what happens. He is quick to tell a woman that he doesn't want to force a relationship.

I don't agree with Mr. Booty Call's ways, but I

applaud the ones that are blunt and do not deceive women to get them in bed. There are some that won't get into a relationship just to get someone in bed, even if his ways are still unacceptable. There are many out there that will take things there. Then they'll proceed to cheat, and treat their partner with disrespect because of a bad decision they made on their own.

<u>He may not take you on many dates, if any</u>

Mr. Booty Call has one thing on his mind regarding you, and it's definitely not spending money unless he feels like he has to. He will more than likely not take you on dates during your fling. He doesn't want to put too much effort into getting sex from you. He also doesn't want you to get the wrong idea, and begin thinking you're more important to him than you really are. He would prefer a discreet and simple sex-filled relationship without all the extra effort. Some of them may take you out in the beginning to speed up the time it takes to win over your panties.

The concept of dates is a debate amongst many women of all age ranges. Many of the women today feel that dating isn't necessary, whereas dates were a major part of courtship in the earlier times. A man was required to not only take you out to a nice place, but he also was required to display his affection for you in respectful ways, such as coming to the door to pick you up, being respectful and greeting your parents, etc. We'll get into that later.

Some women tend to blow dates off as no big deal

99

when they are dealing with the likes of a man they know isn't interested in them as they want him to be. It's an excuse to help them cope with being treated in a less than favorable manner. <u>If a man is interested, he will take you on dates.</u> It doesn't have to be a daily thing, but it does need to exist. Don't get into the habit of lowering your standards to accommodate Mr. No Good.

<u>He only spends time with you if sex is involved</u>

It's completely unacceptable for a man to only come around when he knows he is going to have sex with you. That isn't a healthy relationship, and it's not fair that you are being used only for sexual gain. So many women try to pretend that this type of arrangement is okay because they're getting something out of it too, but it's not. His behavior is only showing you how much you're worth to him.

Anyone that is claiming interest needs to show it. Anyone can lie down and have sex. Even animals have sex. You should expect and demand quality time with someone you're dating, even more so if you're giving up the goods to that person. This should exist before you even have sex, if you value your worth.

It's sad. Many women brag about their partners for the wrong reasons nowadays. Instead of being respected and cherished, they boast about how much money their partner makes, how good in bed they are, or how good they look. Then they wonder why they can never find a good man weeks or months later. Take your focus off of how good he can make you feel sexually, and start to pay attention to how he makes you feel emotionally. The way he treats you as a woman should always outweigh the way he serves you up in the bedroom.

<u>His interest in you declines after sex</u>

If you haven't experienced this, you more than likely will, or you're already experiencing it, and are just choosing to ignore it. Like any hunter or true athlete, Mr. Booty Call likes to be challenged. Of course, they'll take the easy wins, but their attention will be diverted as soon as something else appealing comes along. There's not too much appealing about a woman that will easily give their body to another. The only stand out thing about this behavior to Mr. Booty Call is the convenience. He will continue to call when he wants the convenient sex, because he knows yours is easy to get, and ready whenever he wants it. The only thing is, while he's doing this, he's chasing the next chick who hasn't given it up to him yet.

His attention lies with the woman that's not putting out. He's giving her the attention he once gave you. Then you're stuck wondering what changed, or what pushed him away, and this usually ends in you turning the chase on him. Now you're calling and texting, trying to get his attention back, and becoming more unappealing to him because you seem needy and desperate. You have to make up in your mind whether you want to have sex buddies for the rest of your life, or a fulfilling relationship.

Chapter 9- Mr. Freshly Single

Mr. Freshly Single is the guy who just recently got out of a relationship or marriage, whether it was on his own terms, or someone else's. He may not seem like a part of the Mr. No Good category, but he's not a good option to date at this time.

This guy can fall on either side of the spectrum. He may be ready to treat women as they are supposed to be treated, but the new status as a "free man" may cause him to become a Mr. Ladies' Man. The circumstances of the breakup can make or break his potential to be a good candidate. It's best to give him time to figure things out and actually move on, rather than jump into something with him right away.

Everyone needs time to accept changes in their life for what they truly are, especially breakups. Mr. Freshly Single may be experiencing confused, mixed feelings about his new ex, and what he actually wants to do next. His confusion can cause him to jump into another situation headfirst, act out and become a ladies' man, or even decide he wants his ex back. You don't want to be the one left feeling used or getting played if this kind of situation occurs, so it would be smart and less stressful to let him be for now.

Characteristics of Mr. Freshly Single

- He may still be sad from the break up
- He may be overly anxious to get into a new relationship
- He is still hooking up with his ex
- He may vent about the past relationship often
- He may be a ladies' man, and not be into anything serious

He may still be sad about the break up

This is the most obvious reason why Mr. Freshly Single is no good for you. No one can erase their feelings for someone the day they break up, no matter how much we wish things were this easy. The heart isn't capable of that kind of recovery speed (it would be nice, though). Mr. Freshly Single still has feelings for his ex if they just recently broke up, although he may not behave like he does. He may not admit it, but the feelings are definitely still there. Whether an overwhelmingly strong feeling or a faded one, the feelings still exist. Therefore, it wouldn't be fair to you to pursue something before he completely gets over her. This guy can't focus on having something special with you, when his heart hasn't completely recovered from his past.

Think of Mr. Freshly Single as a door of emotions. Because his feelings are so fresh and the life change is so new, his emotional door is open. An open door can serve many purposes, but these two are the most important: he can walk back through it (returning to his ex, or trying to), and she can walk through it (his ex may return to work things out).

Until he closes that door, those situations have a high possibility of existing. This is why you should always remember the old saying "Don't open a new door before you close the other". You'll avoid potential disappointments if you give him time to close the door. You don't want to be used as a rebound fling that converts to his side woman when he runs back to his old girlfriend.

<u>He may be anxious to get into a relationship</u>

At first glance, the idea of a guy that is ready for a relationship is a good look, many women's dream. However, be careful with this guy because he has his own agenda. Mr. Freshly Single may have an urge to rush into a relationship in order to make his ex jealous. The break up may have left him feeling insecure, especially if he's the one that was dumped. He wants to show his ex that he can keep it moving, and make her think the break up didn't bother him, when actually the break up did just that. This behavior shows obvious signs that he needs time to heal. **Anyone that acts in ways to get some kind of rise or response from their ex has not yet closed that emotional door.** Don't fall for this and become a part of his game.

Another reason Mr. Freshly Single rushes into a new relationship could be because he's not used to being alone, and needs to maintain that feeling he had with his ex. This is a result of insecurity. He may have taken a shot or two to his pride in losing the relationship, and needs an ego boost. So he jumps into a new relationship while he figures out what he really wants. Why does this work? It is because he gets no break in getting attention, support, and intimacy. Some of these guys can easily become Mr. Unavailable.

A lot of freshly single guys will immediately jump into the dating game, and begin taking advantage of being on the market again. They don't want to focus on what was. They just want to have fun to take their minds off of her. Don't end up being one of the rebound flings.

He may still be trying to hook up with his ex

Mr. Freshly Single usually gets to a point where he misses his ex, and may go back to either work things out, or he will continue to sleep with her. This is convenient for him, because he gets to have the best of both worlds. He gets to sleep with her with no obligations, and still pursue you. This is why giving him the time to figure out what he wants is so important. You don't want to be in the middle of that kind of situation, because you're selling yourself short of the undivided attention you could be getting elsewhere, or from him, once he's moved on from his past. What's the rush anyway? If he's such a catch, time and healing will only make him a better man. At this stage, there's not much he can offer you wholeheartedly.

He may vent about his last relationship often

You will more than likely end up playing one of two positions when dating Mr. Freshly Single: the women's advocate or the counselor. He may be completely bitter about his last relationship, and think all women are the same, calling his ex names and cursing all women. You'll spend a lot of time defending women, and having sexist-charged debates until you get annoyed with him. This behavior usually stems from the break up not going in his favor, or her doing something horrible to him, like cheating.

In playing the counselor, he may spend a lot of time venting about the last relationship, including what happened to cause the break up, getting input on where it all went wrong, or halfway in tears realizing he wants her back. This is a very awkward situation to be in, and it isn't fair that you have to counsel him about her during the time that should be spent developing a bond with you. However, this is a direct consequence of you not allowing him time to heal.

Notes

_____

_____

_____

_____

_____

_____

Chapter 10- Mr. Moocher

This guy is definitely one you should stay away from. He is determined to get by in life without working too hard, and will take advantage of any and everybody he can in order to do so. Mr. Moocher believes that others should provide for him, or at least he acts like it. There are a lot of guys today that are refusing to accept man's traditional role of being the provider. Instead, they latch on to independent women, or women that have something of value to offer them, such as money, a place to live, food, drugs, or gifts. Mr. Moocher is out to use you in order to live comfortably.

Guys like this are more likely to prey on women that have something going for themselves. They prefer women that may have their own place, their own car, and a decent job. They may target women who come from wealthy families. There are also some that will go after women that utilize government assistance, because they can benefit from that as well. They know that they can eat as much as they want while staying with a woman that receives food stamps. He also knows that he's likely to get cash and gifts out of a woman that gets extra money, such as a disability or settlement check. This is sad behavior, but that is reality. Mr. Moocher thrives off of women with benefits.

Characteristics of Mr. Moocher

- He may be unemployed often
- He may have lazy qualities
- He has money, but gets it in unstable ways

- He would rather hustle than work
- He may always get money from you
- He may only show up and spend time when your paycheck comes or when you have money
- He may live with other relatives or with friends so that he doesn't have to pay rent

He may unemployed or underemployed most of the time

Mr. Moocher usually either doesn't have a job at all, or he doesn't have one that pays much. This doesn't mean that every man that's unemployed is a moocher. However, after about 3 or 4 months, there's no excuse for a man to still be sitting around singing the woes of how hard it is to find a job, instead of busting his butt to find one. If he remains out of work after a long period of time, he's grown comfortable with his unemployment status, and may not be searching too hard for work. His goal may be to see how long he can get by on using others.

He may have a job, but it may not pay too much. He may just be working a job just to have a little spending money in his pocket, or just to keep his partner or those around him from getting upset with him about not working. Mr. Moocher might go and find a temporary job placement agency to be employed with, and work jobs here and there. He's not looking for anything that will overwork him, or require too much of him, because his goal is ultimately to avoid working unless he absolutely has to.

He may seem lazy

Mr. Moocher not only tries to avoid work, but he also may try to avoid daily responsibilities. He doesn't really want to clean up, babysit, or do much for anyone, including the woman he's getting benefits from. He feels that his presence should be enough. He often tries to compensate his sex for taking care of his woman. Mr. Moocher feels that if he's tearing it up in the bedroom, she should excuse the fact that he's not working. He may not ever say that, but if you pay attention, his actions show it. Whenever his partner complains or gets upset, he tries to make things right with sex or quality time.

He may have money, but it's unstable

Mr. Moocher is more than likely getting benefits from others, not just you. He normally will hang out where he knows he can get a meal, and possibly hang out with those he knows always have something to smoke or sip on. He's not unfamiliar with bumming cigarettes and/or beer. He works his resources for what he needs, whether it is a ride, a few bucks, using someone's cell phone when his is off, and so forth. He normally keeps some kind of money in his pocket due to family members or his lady friends. With enough of this behavior, he begins to feel like he doesn't really have to work so much, especially if he's a ladies' man with quite a few women in rotation.

He would rather hustle than work

Some moochers get involved in selling drugs or other

things to make quick money. However, they may not make as much as they need day by day, so they depend on using others to make up where they lack. Many others simply prefer their daily hustling of food, money, a place to stay, and sex to actually getting a job. They prefer to run the streets, utilizing their options.

There are two guys that I know (they'll be nameless, due to this story) that would go out literally every night of the week. They were both unemployed, so they would only go to bars and clubs where their buddies were bouncers, so they could get in and drink for free. I always used to see them or hear about them going home with different girls each night, and I always wondered how and why they behaved in this manner. I remember thinking that it can't be that serious, to have sex with a different chick every night. I finally found out that the two were practically homeless at the time, living back and forth between buddies because they couldn't get their own place without a job. They were going home with different women nightly in order to get a meal, have sex, and a bed to sleep in, so that they didn't have to crash on their friends' couches every night, or on the floor. They even kept their clothes in the trunks of their cars, just in case the ladies would let them stay for a few days. This is not the kind of guy you want to end up with, ladies. If he can't do for himself, he won't be able to do for you.

He's always getting money from you

Mr. Moocher will more than likely ask you for money

on a normal basis. It might not be an extreme amount, but the request will be made often. Most of the time, it's $10 and $20 here and there, but if he knows you're able, he may ask for more than that. He knows that he can't go overboard with asking, because then it will be obvious what he's up to. **You should never get comfortable with taking care of a man financially.** There's no excuse why he can't get out there and work just as much, if not more, than you do. It is okay to help your man out, but you shouldn't be paying for everything, and especially not his habits, such as drinking, smoking, or going out. You also shouldn't be giving him gas money or letting him use your car all the time if he's not working, and just letting him rip and run in your car. If he's not working, he should at least be spending working hours looking for a job.

Part II.

So you've pinpointed Mr. No Good.....now what?

Chapter 11-One step closer

So you've come to the conclusion that you have a Mr. No Good, or a few of them, in your life. Maybe you've encountered more than one type, maybe you're dealing with one that possesses traits of different types. Either way, hopefully the first section of the book helped you to pinpoint things that are no good for the healthy relationship you desire, and will help you to avoid these types of men from now on.

Now that you're able to distinguish between good men and Mr. No Good, it's time to get to the root of your problems. This is a time to come to terms with your situation, whether it's a marriage, long term relationship, or just a tendency you have to always choose no good men in the dating world.

Considering external factors

Sometimes there are contributing factors to why some men are no good to date, aside from them just being plain selfish. There are some that may make the choice to remain how they are, however there are some that realize their behavior is wrong, and are working to modify it. This is not an excuse to remain with a man that is no good for you. These are just some circumstances that may help you to understand some of them better.

Maturity levels

It's a given that men mature at a slower level than females. So it's no surprise that a lot of younger men (not all of them) will not be ready to settle down in a fully committed relationship, taking their place as the provider and protector. They may be ready to have a girlfriend, but can't handle being with a woman. There is a difference. Guys that still engage in immature behavior more than likely will not take a committed relationship seriously because they barely take their own lives seriously. These kinds of guys aren't going to necessarily be no good for you forever, most of them will eventually grow up and their views on relationships will change drastically. There's no definite age range, so it's best not to sit around and wait. He will not be sitting around waiting on you.

Upbringing

Due to the huge surge of broken homes, many women have been forced to raise kids on their own. This has a major influence on the child. Some men grow up vowing never to disrespect a woman or abandon her, because they empathize with what their own mother goes through day by day. Then you have others that feel that their mother raised them with no father around consistently, making them feel that it's no big deal for other kids to be raised the same way.

A less than ideal upbringing can onset a vicious cycle that can be extremely difficult to break, even for a grown man, if there aren't positive people in his environment demonstrating a positive way to live. Take, for example, a boy that grows up in a home where his father, or his mother's partner, is physically abusive. He continues to view this environment as what love consists of. So when he gets old enough to date, he ends up beating on his partners because it's what he knows best. It's what his environment taught him. No one has told him it's wrong. In fact, he used to see people minding their own business when his mother was abused, enforcing his thoughts that abuse is acceptable in relationships. The same goes for men that may have been raised in homes where their guardians used drugs or drank often. People have to work hard to break these cycles. It all depends on what kind of life he chooses to make for himself.

Knowing when to stay or go

"I don't really wanna stay, I don't really wanna go...what I really need to know is can we get it together?" -702

"Torn in between the two, 'cause I really wanna be with you, but something's telling me I should leave you alone"- Letoya Luckett

These songs hit the nail on the head. There's always mixed emotions when you're involved with someone, or have feelings for someone that isn't treating you right. Embrace the torn feeling though, not because it's the best feeling for you to have, but because it's your heart's way of acknowledging that you deserve better treatment than what you have been receiving.

Should you stay or go? The question has probably popped into your head many times. In most situations, I would say go. **If you've gotten to the point where you find yourself pondering the possibility of leaving a situation, you probably shouldn't be in the relationship.** There is obviously enough trouble on the horizon that is significant enough to make you consider leaving. If you are just beginning to date your guy, this transition should be easy. It's always easier to exit a situation before strong feelings get involved. When you're single, there should be no talk of staying or going. You have nothing tying you to the guys you date, so there shouldn't be a big fuss of whether you should leave the situation.

The dilemma comes into play with long term relationships, mainly marriage. When you marry, you take a vow that you'll remain loyal and bonded to your husband through sickness and health, until death do you part. Many look down upon divorces, and others are afraid of the consequences of them. If you are married to a Mr. No Good, it's important that you do a lot of soul searching to find out if you are yoked to the right person. Marriage is the only situation in which giving a no good man a chance to get it right is deemed acceptable. However, settling for no good behavior is the same as settling down. If your husband is doing something that is harmful to you, and he does not respond to help of any kind, it is probably a safe bet that a separation is needed, so that he can correct his behavior without putting you in harm's way. This doesn't just apply to abusive men. It also includes cheating and substance abuse. However, it is up to you to decide whether a divorce is necessary. **If you're torn on whether to stay or go, it's your conscience telling you what you already know.**

Weighing pros and cons

If you find yourself still unsure of what kind of guy you have, here's another way to figure it out. It's a simple checklist that will help you to see the good (and not so good) qualities of your man. I call it the Breakdown Checklist.

The Breakdown Checklist consists of basic things that Mr. No Good is known for engaging in, as well as things that a good partner does. This list was created after surveying thousands of men and women over a period of 3 months. This isn't a difficult exercise that takes too much thought. As a matter of fact, if you think too much about the options it means you are trying to force your desired outcome, which defeats the purpose of the exercise. Think of the options provided as yes or no questions, so that you won't be forced to explain away the truth.

For example:

"He calls me daily."

Ask yourself if he calls you every day, and if he does, put a checkmark or a "yes" next to it. If he doesn't call you daily, don't say "Well, he calls me enough", "He texts me all the time" or "I don't want him to, but if I did, he would", because that's still a no. This isn't the time to create your ideal guy. It's a time to be real about what's going on in your love life.

Remember, this will help you get a better understanding of how a man should treat you, as opposed to how you may be being treated. If you are just dating, this is a great way to weed out the men who are already showing traits of Mr. No Good in early stages. I have put the Breakdown Checklist on a separate page so that you can tear it out and/or make copies for future reference.

The Breakdown Checklist

Does he:

- Compliment you? _____
- Support your goals and decisions?_____
- Say things that hurt your feelings?_____
- Put down your goals and ambition?_____
- Help you out financially if you need it?_____
- Borrow money from you all the time?_____
- Give you gifts or make special gestures (outside of holidays)? _____
- Remember your birthday and other special days? _____
- Spend a lot of time with you? _____
- Say he's too busy to spend the time you want? _____
- Make an effort to get to know your friends/family? _____
- Make effort for you to meet his family/friends? _____
- Seem happy when he's spending time with you? _____
- Seem bored or aggravated when he's with you? _____
- Take you on dates? _____
- Express his feelings to you? _____

119

- Call you daily (texting excluded)?

  _____

- Text you more than he calls? _____
- Show you affection (sex excluded)? _____
- Only show affection during/before sex? _____
- Respect you? _____
- Make you feel safe and secure? _____
- Make you feel unsafe or uncomfortable? _____
- Spend time with your kid(s) (if applicable)?

  _____

- Seem to not want anything to do with your kid(s)?

  _____

- Live a life of integrity? _____
- Have a spiritual relationship? _____
- Drink/do drugs excessively? _____
- Physically/verbally/mentally abuse you?

  _____

- Hang out with his friends more than you?

  _____

Results

Did the positive outweigh the negative?

_____

Do you feel that you were completely honest
with your answers? _____

Does your partner seem better or worse than you
thought before you completed this checklist?

120

How do you feel about the results?

Thinking back to the answers, do you find a
pattern in the guys you have dated thus far? Do
they all have some of the same qualities?

Beware of Mr. Instant Get Right

In my younger years, I was quite a piece of work. I
know that's hard to believe (yeah right). I was a prankster,
and I was hard headed, always doing things I knew I wasn't
supposed to do. I would get fussed at, and immediately
straighten up my act. It didn't take much of a warning for
me to get some "act right" in my life. Being a knucklehead
was my thing until I was faced with consequences, like a
butt whipping, or having things taken away. All these
consequences were enough to remind me that it was best to
behave for the time being. However, once my parents
weren't around, and the threat of consequence was
removed, I was right back at it. The threat of consequence
became a routine I was no longer afraid of. It wasn't until
my parents actually carried out the consequences that I
learned my lesson.

This behavior still exists today, even in adulthood, for
many people. There are some that do what they're
supposed to do, just because it's the right thing to do. Then

there are others who choose to see how much they can get away with in life, and this behavior carries over into our relationships with others. Mr. Instant Get Right is the poster child for this kind of behavior. He does what he wants to do, even if he knows that his behavior may hurt his partner, and continues to do wrong as long as he can get away with it. He knows that either his partner really has no idea of his wrongdoing, or that she won't really leave him if she finds out.

When Mr. Instant Get Right is found out, he goes into clean up mode. Just like a child changes his or her behavior quickly when threatened with punishment, Mr. Instant Get Right shows a completely different side when faced with the threat of a break up. All of a sudden, the promises of "it'll never happen again" are overflowing, he's showering you with more attention (sometimes even gifts), and he may even reveal a more sensitive side, crying to show remorse.

Be careful of falling into the convincing trap of Mr. Instant Get Right. It can be so easy to see him through rose colored glasses because you want so bad to believe he's truly changed. When someone has developed any type of habit, it can be very difficult and take some time to change their ways. Mr. No Good will not change overnight. You are being unrealistic to think that anyone who is used to satisfying all their selfish needs will immediately remove themselves from that lifestyle.

Cheating, lying, and disrespectful behavior can be just

as much of a problem to Mr. No Good as drugs can be to a drug addict. How often do you see someone that is addicted to drugs and/or alcohol wake up one day and just say they no longer need their fix? It's not that easy, although we'd like it to be. Mr. No Good may mean well when he tells you that he's done doing wrong, but don't be silly enough to expect that change to begin the same day, or even the next one. This belief will set you up for even more heart break, frustration, stress, and possibly a more vicious cycle.

Mr. Instant Get Right is hoping to take the focus off of his wrong doings when he presents his "changed man" speech and behavior. Maybe it's because he can't stand to see you cry, maybe it's because he can't stand to hear you fussing. Either way, he's trying to make things easier for himself. This is also an easy way to avoid consequences. If he pretends he's changed and seen the error in his ways, this helps to reduce the possibility of a break up or any other undesired consequence.

Mr. Instant Get Right is known for being a repeat offender. He understands the power of the "changed man" act and knows that this can keep the right woman there in the relationship. He understands that his partner wants nothing more but for their relationship to work, and he preys on this weakness. When a woman falls into the habit of taking her partner back every time he cheats, or crying and letting it go after an apology is given, this pattern is noticed by her partner. Mr. No Good is an opportunist, and if you keep giving him inches to do you wrong and get to stay out of the doghouse, the behavior and frequency will only increase. And with this increase comes a decrease in happiness and your worth.

The positive results when dealing with Mr. Instant Get Right are only short lived. Sure, he'll begin to be nicer and show you more attention in the time shortly after he is caught. He'll begin doing things to make you happy that he may have never done before. He may go back to doing things he used to do when you first got with him. Some reportedly even go that extra mile in the bedroom during this phase. Don't be so easy to forget the reason he's doing all this making up in the first place. Ask yourself this: if the things he has done never would've been brought to light, would he be trying so hard to make and keep things right?

Chapter 12-Getting him out of your life

So you've finally pinpointed Mr. No Good, and are ready to get him out of your life, once and for all. Let me first say congratulations! So many women get to the point of admitting they have no good men in their lives, but do nothing to get rid of them. It takes courage and a great understanding of self worth to get to this point.

A lot of women want to get rid of toxic partners, but don't know exactly how. It's not always as easy as coming up with a killer line, or throwing a drink in his face and walking off, as reality television and movies make it seem. There's not always a beautiful horse and gorgeous man waiting for you to ride off into the sunset with, and Lord knows we don't need anyone burning clothes and cars like Bernie in Waiting to Exhale!

<u>Creating a plan</u>

The first step to leaving a toxic relationship is to have a plan. This may sound silly, but having a plan in place will help you to think clearly, and it decreases the possibility of you remaining in the relationship, or returning to it.

While working on your plan, there are many things to take into consideration.

Location/Relocation

Kids

Safety

Time

Money

<u>Location/Relocation</u>

In these times, cohabitation or "shacking up" as some call it, is highly common. Many people are choosing to make things easier physically and financially by living together. This can make things a little more difficult for one that is in a toxic relationship. Obviously if you are planning to break up with Mr. No Good, remaining in the same home would be a very unhealthy and possibly dangerous idea.

Consider where you will relocate to. This relocation doesn't have to be permanent, but it does need to be somewhere that is convenient to your time-sensitive situation. If you have a plan in place before you break up with him, this reduces the opportunities for you to be convinced by Mr. No Good to stay, as well as the elimination of opportunities to fight and turn the situation into more of a hostile one.

I once broke up with a boyfriend of years, and we decided that we would both stay until we figured out the next step, since the house was big enough. I wasn't prepared, I didn't have a plan. I just knew that I didn't want to put up with being mistreated any longer. Things went well at first, and we continued to get along because we both worked opposite shifts at our jobs, so we never really saw each other. However, feelings began to get the best of us.

Before I knew it, we had become lovers again, and we were carrying on as if we were still together. The obvious fact that we were not officially together caused things to go downhill. Because of the love we still shared, as well as the house, we couldn't let each other go, even though we both were seeing other people. This brought on huge arguments and jealousy, making our living situation a big mess. The jealousy soon turned into disrespectful acts on both ends, including bringing our dates to the house we shared, and needless to say things kept going downhill from there. This situation could have gotten to the point of being physical, had we not let it go when we did. We had no idea of the seriousness of what we were doing until things got crazy and almost beyond repair. Not only were we in a messy love game, we had selfishly involved others. Aside from the situation having all the makings of a crazy sitcom, it also had the potential to become a violent situation. And to be honest, it was all because I didn't have a plan. I just wanted out.

Knowing where you'll go is probably the most important factor of creating a plan. Getting out of the situation comes first. You can grieve and wonder about all the "who, what, when, where, and why" details later, once you've relocated. In interviewing approximately 195 women about cohabitation and break ups, only 15 of them said that they left immediately after the break up. Within 2 days, they were relocated, as well as all their belongings. These women had a plan. They knew they wanted out, and they acted accordingly. Out of those 15, only 1 of them ended up going back to their ex later on, whereas over 60%

of the women who didn't leave right away eventually when back to their Mr. No Good. Those statistics go to show that women that leave as soon as it's over are more likely not to return to the toxic situation.

Many of the other women had all kinds of excuses to give when asked why they didn't leave right away. Some of them included the following:

- Financial problems
- Shared lease
- Didn't want the kids to know right away
- No place to go
- No vehicle to leave in

While these can be considered legitimate reasons, they are still, in fact, excuses. That is why having a plan in place before the time comes is so important. We are normally well aware of our relationship circumstances, so it should be no surprise when the relationship has pretty much run its course.

Make a list of all the friends and family members you can think of. Don't rule anyone out, because you never know who may be willing to let you stay with them temporarily. Don't automatically expect that friend or family member with a big house to take you in, and don't assume the one with a small studio apartment can't help you. Make some calls ahead of time to secure a place to go. Even if you have to sleep somewhere else and leave your belongings at home, that is better than you physically being there.

Consider your location. Are you close to anyone that you could temporarily stay with? Do you know anyone living in the same state or city as you that could help you out? Your loves can play a big part in helping you get out of this toxic situation.

Other options include moving into your own place, finding a sublease opening, or checking into a hotel. Of course, these options will cost more than rooming temporarily with a friend or family member, but it will still give you an option outside of staying in your current situation.

Time

Time is very important to consider in this situation because it can make or break you. Too much time in the home after you've broken up with Mr. No Good can cause you to begin feeling that things aren't as bad as they really are, or that it is your fault, and that it may be easier for you to remain in your comfort zone.

Give yourself a time frame to work with. This may help you to stick with your plane easier. With a detailed plane, the time frame should be fairly short. If you know where you're headed already, then there shouldn't be much time wasted between breaking up and physically leaving.

Don't get caught up wasting too much time planning either. Remember, this isn't a long term blueprint. It's more of an exit strategy for your current situation. Creating the plan with different options shouldn't take too long, especially if you've already confirmed who you can stay with, and where. The rest is simple, and the details can be figured out once you've gotten to your destination.

Money

Money, and the lack of it, seemed to be the major common denominator amongst over 80% of the women I interviewed regarding breakups and why they stayed. Many of the women I spoke with weren't financially stable enough to just leave at the drop of a dime. Some stated that they had savings account, but that there wasn't enough money in them to book a flight, or gas up to drive to another state. Others stated that their money was in a joint account with their partner, and they were afraid to take out a large amount of money. Some were afraid to lose their money to their partner, afraid that upon him finding out they're about to break up, that he would clean out the bank account.

Money is such a powerful thing. Money can have a major impact on relationships, including being the reason for many break ups. Everyone wants more of it, and no one wants to lose it. Often in destructive relationships, money is used as a form of maintaining control. Mr. No Good may go to extreme lengths of completely controlling finances in order to make sure his partner can't have too much freedom. He can often be the primary breadwinner, or he can control the finances by rationing money to his partner as he sees fit.

Sometimes, it's not even that complicated. Many

women stay in relationships with Mr. No Good because it's simply cheaper to keep him. They begin to think about having to pay their bills alone, having to pay rent, and other financial responsibilities. These things were so much easier to maintain when a partner was paying half or all of it. Freedom from a horrible relationship just doesn't seem worth the tad bit of financial assistance you're currently receiving while with him. Some wonder if they'll even be able to afford living on their own. They begin to think of the lifestyle changes the split will bring.

This is why having a financial plan for yourself is so important. You should never have to remain in an unhealthy situation because of financial reasons. This is especially crucial pertaining to unmarried couples. Without marriage, there are less guarantees of financial obligation. A boyfriend isn't necessarily required to pay your bills, help you with your kids, or start a joint bank account with you. To be blunt, his money isn't your money, and neither is your money his. Therefore, you shouldn't depend on your partner's income to always support you, because you never know what can happen. Relationships aren't guaranteed to last, and neither is employment. It is up to you to be financially prepared in case things take a turn for the worst.

Creating a financial plan

- Save money in a fund/bank account
  - Maintain employment

- Pinpoint friends/family that may be willing to help
- Keep documentation of financial records (especially joint bank accounts)
- Make sure your name is on any accounts you may share with your partner

Money tends to carry a lot of power within relationships, whether some believe it or not. This is especially true when couples begin combining their income. This is why you should always have a separate savings, in case of emergency. It's smart to always have money saved up anyway, but especially when you are combining your money with someone else's. You never know what may happen between the two of you. Relationships, and even marriages, aren't guaranteed to last forever, so you have to be prepared for the "what ifs" at all times.

If you don't have enough money to leave at the time of a breakup, there are few things to consider. If you're working, and you feel safe, you may want to consider remaining until your next paycheck comes in. Then your paycheck can be used to relocate. This isn't an ideal situation, but if you've exhausted all your options of places to stay while you work, then this may be the best option. You don't want to put yourself in a position where going to work is affected, because you could risk losing your job behind your personal life.

Another option is to borrow from a friend or family member. Don't be so sure that no one will be willing to help you out. Also, don't let your pride keep you in an unhealthy situation. If you don't feel comfortable asking for financial help from someone you know, look into short term payday loans. Your first step out of the home you share with your partner doesn't have to be your final one. Square away the temporary relocation before you begin thinking of where you're going to settle down for the rest of your life. Of course, don't borrow more money from anyone or any bank than you're willing to pay back. It will only add to your problems.

Kids

When deciding to end a no good relationship and kids are involved, leaving can be a tad bit more difficult. Some things to take into account are ages of the children, school and extracurricular activities, and whether or not to take them.

It's always important to take into account your kids' ages and how much they do or do not understand. Leaving may cause stress to an older child that is aware of what's going on, and a younger child may display separation anxiety from your partner. It is best to avoid causing a scene or arguing as you leave in order to reduce the stress and confusion it may cause the kids.

Choosing whether or not to take the kids with you is something that needs to be taken into consideration. This may seem like common sense to many, but it can be more complicated than you think. Whether your living situation is with the child's father or with a long term partner, they should definitely leave with you if the situation is an unsafe one. **If you feel threatened, you should never leave your kids with your partner.** You'd be putting your kids in danger by leaving them there with a dangerous partner. Remove your children from this situation as soon as possible.

It is a very touchy subject when discussing a mother and father's battle over the kids, so I won't go too far into it. Only you can decide if you want your kids with you during this time of transition or not. Some may feel that the children should remain in their normal routine until a new place is squared away. Your work schedule may not allow you to take on full time responsibility at the last minute. Before you assume that the answer is always to take your kids, evaluate your situation closely. **Just because a man is no good for the relationship does not mean he is a bad father.** Only you can make this decision, but don't be that woman who takes children away from their dad just because he won't act right for you, and then use them as a pawn throughout the separation.

Another factor to consider is your children's school schedule. If you are planning to relocate, will your children have to transfer schools, or will you still be able to get them there? If your work schedule doesn't allow for you to pick them up and drop them off, is there someone you trust that can help you with their transportation? One thing that shouldn't happen is your kids missing school because of your failure to plan ahead.

Safety

This is not something to play around with. If you feel that you are in a potentially dangerous situation, you need to leave as soon as possible, and also be smart about the situation. Your plan to leave should involve someone else assisting you, whether it be a friend of family member, or even a police escort. If your partner is already showing signs that are unsafe, it is highly possible that he may lose it when you try to leave. It is very important to have a plan in place to make sure you leave safely, and that your partner doesn't know where you're relocating to.

If you have no current place to go, do not be afraid to seek help through a woman's center or shelter until you feel safe. A relationship is never worth physical pain or death, so it is important you do whatever you can to make it to a safe place.

Prepare a support team

Just as friends and family members may play a big part in helping you physically leave Mr. No Good, they should also play a major part in supporting you through this time, and making sure you never look back. Having a support system is very helpful because it can give you a sense of comfort and reassurance in a time that may be stressful. Without anyone in your corner, it may seem easier to stay in your comfort zone, which keeps you settling for an unhealthy relationship.

Everyone is not meant to be a part of your support system. No matter how much you may love your friends and family, everyone won't be helpful. Bringing too many people into the situation will bring too many opinions, which can cause more problems and confusion rather than solutions.

Your support system should definitely include loyal and trustworthy people. If you can't trust him/her on a daily basis with small things, you probably don't need to bring them into this situation. Also, choose people that have always been there for you. Now is not the time to tests out that new girlfriend's loyalty. Remember you are letting these people into a very sensitive area of your personal life.

Make sure that you avoid judgmental people. A judgmental person is the last person you need monitoring your every move, because they're too concerned with telling you what you should've done, what you shouldn't have done, and what they would've done differently or better. This person is more into knowing your business in order to make comparisons. This isn't the kind of person you need around at this time.

Although it may be nice to have an extremely positive friend around, sometimes this can backfire. This person is sure to build you up, and make you feel better about yourself, but they may end up trying to convince you to go back and work things out. Too much positivity can cause some women to be delusional about relationships, therefore they sometimes end up remaining in dead end situations, in hopes that they will get better and eventually become the relationship they desire. This isn't the kind of influence you need while you are walking away from Mr. No Good. Be sure to pick someone who is positive, yet realistic for your support team. It is better that someone talk sensibly rather than filling your head with the "maybe he'll change" talk.

Don't feel obligated to include family in your support system. Although there are many who have supportive families, some can be more damaging. Gauge your family situation and decide what is best for you. There may be one or two family members that you can trust and lean on.

Avoid the "I told you so" people. We all have someone in our life that knows it all, and has no problem letting the world know it. There will always be someone that is right and wrong in how they feel about your relationship, but now is not the time to be lectured and reminded that you were warned about Mr. No Good. Some people are more interested in being right about the situation, rather than helping you out of it. Avoid those people until you are comfortable with speaking to them about the situation. Their negative, condescending attitude will only bring you more sadness, frustration, and embarrassment, hindering you instead of helping you. This person should probably be reevaluated in the friendship category anyway, if she'd rather be right about everything, rather than being your rock.

Possible support team members

_____
_____
_____
_____
_____
_____
_____
_____
_____
_____

- Why did you pick these people?
- Do your team picks support you currently?
- How well do these team members know your situation?
- Will any of them be judgmental?

NOTES

_____
_____
_____
_____
_____
_____
_____
_____
_____
_____

Chapter 13-Executing the plan and not looking back

You've done the behind the scenes work. Doors have been opened up to you, and your support team is in place. The only thing left for you to do now is leave. This may include leaving now and explaining later, or breaking up with him first. However you planned out your escape of this toxic relationship, be sure to stick to your plan as much as possible, and don't second guess yourself. Remember, leaving an unhealthy, unsatisfying relationship is for the best.

Can we talk?

After all the planning and coming to terms with the fact that it's time to let Mr. No Good go, it's finally time to let him know. Ending things can be extremely difficult, and all situations are different, so no general speech can be written. Now is your time to speak from your heart, and speak up for your happiness that has been disregarded.

The importance of this talk is to let your partner know that things aren't working out for you, and that you no longer want to continue this relationship. Be sure to be clear with this, because talking around what really needs to be said will only complicate things and set you back. You've come too far in growth to quit right before you remove yourself from Mr. No Good arms. He needs to understand that you mean it, and that you want more for yourself in love and in life. He needs that understand that the mistreatment has come to an end. Now is not the time to backtrack and sugarcoat your feelings. You have every right to free yourself from unhappiness and unhealthiness.

Mr. No Good will more than likely have a lot to say. He might go into explaining his actions or lack of action. It's okay to hear him out and be considerate, but be sure that you're only hearing his point of view, rather than pushing yourself back into the relationship. Mr. No Good tends to know all the right things to say in order to clean up his wrongdoings and get what he wants. Don't let apologies, tears, and promises convince you to stay in a toxic, dead end situation. Apologies are good (especially when they're sincere), but they don't justify going back to a situation that you're not happy in. Apologies and remorse does not fix relationships. If Mr. No Good did right by you in the first place, there would be no need for apologies and trying to clean up the mess. This moment is not about him. You have been all about him up until this point, looking the other way and attempting to ignore the mistreatment he gives you. This moment is about you, and the happiness you deserve. Don't back out.

You may feel many different emotions during this time. Be prepared to experience sadness, anger, confusion, and even his sadness. Many aren't prepared for the overload of emotions break ups bring, and it sets them back in their progression. It's okay to feel some kind of way when you're ending tings. There's nothing wrong with having feelings. It's how we react to those emotions that may cause problems. Stay strong, and keep your focus on what needs to be done in order for you to move on with your life, and get closer to true happiness.

If words fail you in this time, and you can't think of any of the reasons you've come up with to end things, try this powerful statement.

"You have shown that you can't love or treat me the way I want you to, so it's best that we part ways."

Remember: This is a breakup, which is a break OUT of unhappiness that is needed to break IN to the life and happiness you desire and deserve.

<u>Saying "No" and meaning it</u>

I had many discussions about break ups with men from different backgrounds, some who were admittedly Mr. No Good, and others that treated their partners well. From the single men to the married men, much of the views on breaking up were the same. Most of the men I spoke with couldn't deal with a woman breaking up with them. Many referred to it as a "blow to their ego". Some of them even stated that the decision to end things should lie in the hands of the one that is doing wrong, because they got unhappy with the relationship first. Those men had a "how dare YOU end things when I don't really want to be with YOU" mentality about the break up. The behavior that was present among all of them was that they still reached out to their partner after the breakup, whether they wanted her back or not.

It's no secret. Mr. No Good usually continues to call and text after things are over. He may want to win you back, just to transfer the power back into his hands. He may just want to keep having sex with you. If anyone is going to end things, he feels that it should be him. It's up to you to make sure that you're saying "no", as well as following up your words with actions.

You've come too far to still be giving into a guy that has proven he's not willing to do what it takes to keep you happy. Don't ruin all your hard work by turning back. Get comfortable with saying "no" to Mr. No Good. Let me rephrase that. Don't just get comfortable with saying "no", get comfortable with meaning it.

If you feel uncomfortable with something, or feel that you will regret your actions later, don't engage in it. If Mr. No Good is inviting you over to "talk", just say no. Deep down, you know that's what you should be saying, but it can feel uncomfortable at first, because you are so used to giving in to him. Step out of your comfort zone and into a zone where you value your self respect more than pleasing someone who doesn't value you.

Before you make a decision to start communicating or hanging out with him again, think about all the reasons you let Mr. No Good go in the first place. Sometimes, it's that reminder that is needed to keep you moving ahead. He doesn't deserve your time, and you shouldn't waste time explaining why you don't want to be with him over and over again. Don't let him talk you back into being involved with him, or wasting any more energy on him. Say no, and follow it up with ignoring his attempts to suck you back in.

He will eventually realize you're serious.

Reasons we hold on

Everyone has different reasons why they feel that hanging on to Mr. No Good is okay. Plenty of songs, new and old, explain the "benefits" of having a piece of man around, making it appear to be the smartest thing to do. Coming to terms with the real reasons you want this man to remain in your life is a great way to pinpoint your own insecurities, and begin to change in order to acquire real happiness. You cannot move forward into regaining self worth without first understanding and acknowledging and acknowledging what compromised it in the first place.

Sunshine and Rainbows

If you're anything like me, you try to see good in all things. However, there is a line that must be drawn between drawing positives from all circumstances, and overlooking the negatives completely to continue to benefit from positives. I like to call the latter the "Sunshine and Rainbows" mentality. People with this mentality may know something is wrong, but will completely ignore the problem, no matter how big, and hang on to whatever positives they can find. If you think like this, you are more than likely cancelling out the bad things your partner says and does with the few good qualities he may possess, or ones you have created for him.

When you fall into this category, you have clearly gotten to the point that you are more engaged with his potential, or the way things used to be, rather than what is going on right now. He may have charmed you in the beginning to win you over, and the hope that this charming guy will return fuels you to continue in the relationship. Often women get so caught up in what their partner could be that they ignore what their partner is. That untapped potential you are seeking may not even exist in him. This can be confusing, because Mr. No Good can be charming, intelligent, and have a way with words. He does not always come in the form of a complete jerk or monster. It can be easy at times to conveniently outweigh his bad qualities with the good ones he possesses in order to feel justified in staying.

Desperate for love

Many people take the word "desperate" and associate it with images of skanky women, and even older attention-seeking women. Over the years the word "thirsty" has been used as an interesting substitute. However, many never realize that their own behavior can be that of an individual that is desperate for love.

So many women long for the experience of love and the feeling of being adored, so much that it tends to cloud their judgment. No matter what your background story, we all tend to crave love. The difference is the extent to which one may desire it. Some women crave love they may have never experienced, love they simply didn't get enough of in the past, or even just drama-free love. These women cross the line of needing love into being desperate for it.

A woman that is desperate for love will often tolerate unhealthy relationships in order to continue to possess a piece of what she desires. Usually most people who are desperately seeking love are those who may have psychological and emotional needs that are unmet, sometimes dating all the way back to childhood. It's easier for someone who's never really experienced love to crave it in an eager way. Desperation for love is the reason many women stay in unhealthy relationships with the first person they've ever been with, abusive men, and even guys they know are being unfaithful. Some call this behavior having a "hungry heart".

This act of desperation sometimes doesn't just apply to the need for love, but also to the need to be in a relationship, no matter how the woman is being treated. Many different women have stated that they feel empty and/or incomplete when they're not in relationships. There are probably thousands more who feel this way, but won't admit it. This is one of the main signs that you're in love with the thought of being in a relationship more so than the person you're with.

Another sign is when you find yourself dating one guy after another, not really leaving any downtime to give yourself a break. Sadly, many women have developed the idea that you are not desirable if you're not in a relationship. 85% of the women interviewed in the writing of this book deemed being single as a punishment. People that feel this way feel that a relationship defines you. Get rid of this self-defeating mentality. You are not giving yourself enough credit if you feel that you're only valuable with someone else by your side.

What will they say?

We'd be liars if we said it never crossed our minds. When break ups happen, it seems like everyone all of a sudden has an opinion, and wants to pass judgment. Since elementary school, this has seemed to be the way of the world. Everyone has their own view of why things ended, and whose fault it was. Therefore, naturally we tend to feel embarrassed of what people may begin to say or do once the break up news gets out. This fear of humiliation can cause even the most confident women to be afraid of taking the step to leave a relationship, especially those that have been in a long term one. As much as we like to pretend we couldn't care less what others think about us, the truth is peer pressure still plays a major part in relationship direction.

Break ups tend to be viewed negatively, almost as if it's personal failure, sometimes even when you're leaving your partner for good reason. People automatically assume that because you're breaking up with someone, you must have not been able to hold things together, or keep him happy. Thoughts such as these invade your brain as well, making you even more paranoid about the whole situation. Because of this wide spread public judgment and exposure of a once private matter, many women choose to stay in unhappy and destructive relationships rather than face the rest of the world and their judgment.

"Clean up woman"

If you're not familiar with Betty Wright's popular song "Clean up Woman", I'll go ahead and explain this to you. However, I strongly recommend you check out this song in your free time, it's a great classic. The "Clean up woman" is known for being the woman your man runs to for some of the following reasons.

- When he's feeling unappreciated
- When he's unhappy with the relationship
- When he's horny and just wants some variety
- When the relationship's pretty much over

The "Clean up woman" seems to possess all of the things you don't, or at least he feels that way. She has no problem competing with you for your man, and taking him in once you leave him. I'm sure you can name a few women that are like this.

Now that you have a good idea of who she is, you can see how much of an impact other women can have on your relationship, if you choose to allow that. So many women choose to stay with Mr. No Good just to keep him from being available to other women. This becomes an unspoken competition between women that may not even know much about each other. All that you know is that you don't want this chick "winning" your man over. So instead of leaving him to capitalize on your deserved happiness, you stay and sacrifice it just to keep him out of the arms of another woman.

Since I was younger, I've always heard women giving others the same advice. "Girl, don't let that woman have what you worked so hard to have/keep!" From older women to women's roles in movies, society has taught women to fight to keep their men, no matter what they've been through with him. We've been taught to make sure the "other" woman doesn't win. Have you ever taken the time to think about what's really being "won"? This way of thinking focuses more on the other woman than it does on Mr. No Good himself. Are you really losing something special by letting go of a man who isn't treating you like he should? Who cares if he runs to her after you leave him? Would you rather keep him and put up with the miserable relationship of allowing disrespect, lying, and health risk, all while he's still running to her?

Here's the truth: **Staying with a cheating man or a man that you know no longer wants to be with you is a setup for more heart break.** He's not going to stop cheating, and he'll only do it more because your decision to remain lets him know he can continue to get away with it. **Staying will not make him love or respect you more.** Do you want more truth? **The "Clean up woman" isn't going anywhere.** She will stay entertaining your man as long as he allows her to. It's more challenging for her to eventually get him away from his woman. Someone has to respect themselves enough to get out of this potentially dangerous love triangle. Why not let it be you?

Remember: the "Clean up woman" isn't thinking about the fact that he may repeat the same no-good behavior with her. It's a losing situation for both women involved. No one will get respect until the disrespecting denominator is out of the question.

Who will want me now? (Self image)

Over the course of a destructive relationship, feelings of unattractiveness and low self-concept tend to drastically develop. Women tend to automatically deem themselves as unworthy of love, unattractive, and unworthy of happiness because of the way they have been treated by Mr. No Good. Not only does this self-defeating mentality arise, it is also often cosigned by destructive men who aim to keep their women at bay by making them feel undesirable. These men feed their women statements such as these:

- "No other man will want you."
- "I'm the only guy that would ever put up with you."
- "You're ugly."
- "You're too big/skinny."
- "You have too many issues to ever find a better man."
- "You're worthless."
- "You're nothing without me."

150

Often Mr. No Good makes these kinds of statements in hopes that his woman will never want to even try to date anyone else, even after he's out of the picture. This behavior is a result of his own insecurities, but women tend to focus more on the hurtful words being spoken rather than looking into the reason those things are said. We are emotional creatures, and it's amazing how much more susceptible we are to insults rather than compliments. A man can tell us we're beautiful every day, and we write it off as empty flattery or insincerity. However, he may say something hurtful one time, and it hangs out in the back of our minds forever.

For this reason, women in destructive relationships hold onto their Mr. No Good because they feel that if they leave, they'll be lonely for a long time, if not forever. They are afraid that if their man feels that they're not good enough, surely other men will feel the same way. Have you ever experienced these feelings?

No relationship is worth the loss of your self esteem. Self love is crucial for true happiness. Without knowing your own worth, you cannot even begin to truly love another person. The minute your partner's negative views of you become your own, you should know that changes need to be made. When you don't feel good about yourself, it's hard to make anyone else happy, which defeats the purpose of remaining in a relationship. Being with someone should never make or break you.

Fear

Another common reason why women hang onto Mr. No Good is the presence of fear. Fear can be a powerful control tool, not just used by him to control, but also as a trap you've set for yourself. Your fear of how he will react contributes to your hesitancy to leave.

It's clear that Mr. No Good doesn't want you to leave. They lose that sense of control when you get the courage to leave him behind. This is one of the biggest threats you could ever pose to him. This fear of Mr. No Good's anger has a way of keeping you in line, and making you think twice about taking that significant step.

Fear of leaving a toxic relationship is very understandable and common. Mr. No Good, especially Mr. Abusive, tends to step up his methods of control when he senses his partner has made the decision to get out of the relationship. It's his way of saying "I'm not going down without a fight". Sometimes physical abuse is the desperate measure Mr. No Good takes. More common desperation measures include verbal abuse and intimidation, in hopes that you feel you're not good enough to find anyone else.

Getting over your fear takes courage and confidence. It's not easy and does take mental and emotional preparation. If you feel threatened, and you're afraid that Mr. No Good may become abusive and/or harass you upon deciding that you want out of the relationship, do not be afraid to have police or friends/family members be there to assist you with leaving safely. Don't be afraid to get an injunction if you feel it is necessary.

Notes

_____

_____

_____

_____

_____

_____

_____

_____

_____

_____

_____

_____

_____

_____

_____

_____

_____

_____

_____

_____

Chapter 14-Surviving the side effects

When a break up occurs, especially with long term relationships, there are many side effects that can make things difficult. To remove something or someone that has been a very significant part of your life can be extremely emotional. You will more than likely experience one or more of these common issues: embarrassment, sadness, loneliness, and financial setbacks.

Embarrassment

Often when a relationship doesn't work out, many that were familiar with the relationship wonder and ask why. It's very rare that breakups happen without anyone noticing, and this can cause embarrassment. Most people don't want the world to know when things go wrong, and they feel a break up is viewed as a failure to keep it together. Don't let embarrassment make you feel that you did the wrong thing. Many others have gone through the same issues. Stand proud in your decision to get rid of someone who doesn't deserve to be in your life. What's more embarrassing is to remain in a relationship with someone you and everyone else know isn't treating you with respect. Wouldn't you rather be the one that respected herself enough to leave?

Who cares if people know the relationship didn't work out? Most of the people you are worried about may already know that he wasn't any good in the first place. The bottom line is this: people will discuss you whether you're doing well or horribly. **Don't let what other people say and**

think about you hinder you from leaving a toxic situation to find true happiness. Most of the people that are busy discussing your relationship problems usually have just as many of their own. They disguise that by emphasizing other people's problems .

Remember that love and dating is not a race to happiness. You are not in competition with other couples, so stop comparing yourself to others that are in relationships. You may never know all the ups and downs of their situation, just as they don't know yours.

Loneliness

You may feel extremely lonely now that you're no longer in a relationship. You're probably used to having him around, or even just the fact that you had someone you could call yours. This can leave you feeling empty, and longing for your partner's company.

Don't let this feeling of loneliness lead you back into the arms of Mr. No Good. It can be easy in this vulnerable time to rush into another situation before you're ready, and it may not be with a better partner choice. Often women tend to fall for guys with similar qualities of their exes, especially when there's a fresh break up. How often have you dated someone that reminds you of your ex? Have you ever found yourself saying "If I could take _____'s good qualities and put them with _____, he'd be perfect"? We tend to hang onto our "type", and also the good memories of our former lovers.

You have to learn to establish the difference between being alone and being lonely. Sure, everybody wants someone, but you need to be content standing alone instead of jumping from one situation to the next, or back into the last one. Use this time that you're alone to learn more about yourself and what happiness means to you. We'll get into that later. Keep pushing ahead. Now that you've taken that major step, you are on the right path to better days and happiness.

Physical side effects

Although it may be obvious to some, many don't realize how much of a toll unhealthy relationships can take on your body mentally, emotionally, and physically. Relationship choices, internal and external, can take your body through major changes. Staying in an unhealthy relationship is the same as practicing unhealthy habits, such as smoking, unprotected sex, and eating unhealthy foods. It may be suitable for now, but overall your health and longevity are being majorly compromised.

Exhaustion

Many don't understand exactly how mentally and physically exhausting a relationship with Mr. No Good really is. So much energy is spent on being pulled in different directions just to keep the relationship together. Part of you is trying to figure out how you can change to make him happier. Part of you is trying to keep everything perfect in order to keep him from getting upset. A bunch of energy is put into trying to figure out what he's doing behind your back, and who he's doing it with. All these things are stressful and exhausting to the mind, not even including all the emotions you experience because of his actions. This kind of emotional burnout can cause you to be more fatigue, lazy, and/or unmotivated. Studies show that unhappy people sleep more hours than happy people. This could be due to all the stress and turmoil in relationships causing burnout. Sleeping could also be a way that people in unhealthy relationships temporarily escape their issues.

Hypertension

You probably see people joking about someone's actions making their blood pressure go up, but there is a lot of truth to that statement. When you're too excited, angry, or worked up about something, your blood pressure can creep higher and higher, causing major health issues. Hypertension is a leading health issue, and most of the time it is associated with eating habits and weight. However stress can send your blood pressure soaring sky high, just as much as high sodium intake.

Cold turkey

If you were sexually involved with your partner, then it's a safe bet that you will begin to miss those intimate moments eventually. We're human, and those needs don't just disappear into thin air as soon as a break up happens. However, the longing to physically be with Mr. No Good gets many women into trouble. It is when we begin to think we can still have a sexual relationship with the ex that major problems and confusion arise.

Don't find yourself back in Mr. No Good's bed after you take the major step to get him out of your life. It's the easiest way to destroy all the hard work and confidence you've built up in this time. Nothing good will come out of sleeping with your ex, other than temporary satisfaction. It may seem worth it at the time, but it only leaves you with mixed feelings and sometimes even shame and regret. Why do something that you know you'll beat yourself up over later? Why continue to give Mr. No Good power over you? Sure, you can convince yourself that you're in control of the arrangement and your emotions, but the truth is he's still in control if he can still keep having sex with you after not even treating you right during the relationship. After all, Mr. No Good showed with his actions that he didn't value you enough to keep you happy and treat you right, but now he still gets to have your body and heart?

Doesn't sound like you're winning, does it? Have enough respect for yourself not to continue giving a special part of yourself to someone who didn't treat you like you were special enough.

Don't think that you'll be able to move on and gain happiness while you're still your ex's booty call. You owe it to yourself to steer completely clear of Mr. No Good. Too much emotion and mind games are intertwined in sexual arrangements for you to be able to balance that as well as moving on. Which is more important to you, sex here and there, or valuing your self-worth and moving on with your life to find the one that will give you happiness and respect?

Tip: Stay out of the "friend zone" for a while. So many people seem to think that exes can be friends, and that is true in some cases. However, with a fresh break up, it's best to keep some distance for a while. Feelings are still strong, and this can be an extremely vulnerable time for you. Don't convince yourself that you can end things and go right into being strictly friends. That's not easy, and it is only an excuse for you to keep him around. Now is the time to focus on you and moving ahead. Trying to build a friendship while feelings are still involved can be problematic for all involved, and can seriously halt your plans of truly letting Mr. No Good go.

Part III
Getting Real with Yourself

This section is all about you. Mr. No Good is out of the picture, but there is still work to be done. These toxic men don't always enter your life by chance. There is obviously something that attracts you enough to give these types of men access into your heart and life. Therefore a major part of removing the toxic men out of your life and keeping them away is owning up to the reasons they were there in the first place, and taking responsibility, for allowing yourself to be treated in a disrespectful and careless manner.

The remaining work includes learning why you behave and think the way you do, because it goes hand in hand with activating your self esteem and realizing your self-worth. It's time self-worth takes center stage so that Mr. No Good won't be able to make guest appearances in your life anymore.

Now is the time to focus on you and only you. All this time you have been playing second fiddle to your lovers' happiness, and neglecting yours. It's time to take the driver's seat and coast into the happiness you deserve! But first, you must begin to understand yourself.

Many women go through life blaming the men in their life for their unhappiness and attributing their bitter demeanor to the lack of good men in the world, but the truth is this: You have complete control over your happiness. A person can only change your attitude and outlook on your life if you allow them to.

Having self esteem and understanding your worth is

extremely important in order for any relationship to work, and this section will help you understand the significance of loving yourself, and understand why you deserve more than what you've put up with thus far.

We will also take a look into your life's patterns in hopes that you can release some of your past circumstances and understand how your past can sometimes play a significant part in your adult relationships today.

This section may not be the easiest to go through. Many sensitive topics will be covered, and you will be forced to face some truths that may sting a little, but coming to terms with the root of the issue will help you in the long run, not just with relationships, but with life's circumstances in general.

Take as long as you need with this section until you're comfortable enough to keep moving forward. Refer back to this section as much as you need to.

Chapter 15-Where it all began

In order to begin to fully understand yourself and why you are who you are today, it is important to acknowledge your past. Many people go through life with characteristics that they don't understand, but they never look to their past to get an answer. The recent past is as far as many people like to go. Looking into your past will shed a lot of light on your present life patterns, often in ways you never would've thought about.

Childhood

Relationships have existed in your life since the day you were born. The bond with your mother started while you were in the womb. Relationships with siblings developed as you got older. As you aged, you began to establish relationships with peers. Childhood can play a major part in your life today, as it can have an effect on your interpersonal relationships.

What do you remember about your childhood? Were you a happy child? Were you outgoing or introverted? Did you get in trouble a lot, or did you behave well most of the time? Studies show that happy kids end up with more successful relationships in their adulthood. Children that are withdrawn seem to lack the social skills they need to establish successful relationships. The introverted demeanor sometimes carries over into adulthood when it's not corrected, causing issues in many different areas of life.

You don't have to remember your childhood for it to

have an effect on your life. Although we tend to mature, some of our traits we had as children stick with us well into adulthood. If you aren't familiar with your childhood, ask your parents and/or siblings about it. They may be able to give you insight on your personality, your attachment patterns, and your temperament.

Parenting traits

Many of the things we long for in adulthood are a result of the lack of that very thing while we were growing up. Parenting comes into play as we begin to look at what existed and what was missing as far as love and attention is concerned.

Indifferent parents

Were your parents unresponsive while you were growing up? Did they seem to not care about anything as long as you stayed out of big trouble? You may have spent your days doing things to get your parents' attention and affection without realizing the effect it had on you. Unresponsive parents tend to bring on an attention seeking mentality. You want to be noticed, and feel loved, to the point where it may cause you to make poor decisions just to get those feelings satisfied.

This situation causes the desperate need for attention and affection in your adult life. You may find yourself auditioning and trying to move towards a relationship with most of the guys you meet, in hopes that you can win somebody's heart over. There is a strong desperation to please and keep everything seemingly perfect so you won't feel unappreciated or lonely. With this longing for attention comes the longing for affection. You may need raw affection shown to you all the time in order to feel that he is into you. You may need to be hugged, kissed, and sexually involved all the time to feel that someone cares about you. This behavior is easily preyed upon by Mr. No Good, but it can also run guys off. Desperation is never a good quality in relationships.

Absent parents

Were your mother and/or father missing from your life growing up? Were they unable to parent you due to incarceration, drugs, alcohol, or death? An absent parent can play a major part in your interactions today. More often kids are being raised in single parent homes, but it doesn't take away from the fact that both mother and father qualities are needed to effectively raise a child.

When the mother is absent, the nurturing and displays of lady like behavior are missing. Daughters that grow up without good mother figures don't always grasp the nurturing and feminine qualities they need in order to show respectful and appropriate affection in their adult years. Often the affection is translated into casual sex with others, because they weren't able to see love and affection in their own household.

An absent father can be extremely detrimental to females. A positive father figure demonstrates protection, love, and provides for his family, so the absence of this demonstration while growing up can lead women into the hands of toxic men. You may be searching for the love you never got from a father figure. This can cause women to lean towards men that are controlling and/or abusive. You may also date specifically for financial support. With no father around to show how a man should treat a woman, a woman can easily mistake mistreatment for love.

Powerful fathers

A powerful father can have major influence on women growing up as well. Sometimes the image of a powerful father can cause women to over idealize. You may begin to feel that no one is good enough because they don't measure up to your father. This can cause unrealistic views on love and relationships, and run off guys that could be potential mates.

Understand this: No man will ever be able to make up what you lacked while growing up. Your partners aren't there to replace daddy or play the daddy you never knew. It's not fair to hold them to this expectation. Expecting this will continue to leave you disappointed. There needs to be a definite separation of father and partner roles. Or else you will always have conflict, even in promising relationships.

Your experiences growing up with or without a father need to be fully understood so that you can move forward without those subconscious expectations that damage your adult relationships.

166

NOTES

- What was your childhood like?
- Were both parents active in your life?
- Did you ever feel unappreciated/unloved growing up?
- If a parent was absent, how did it make you feel? Do you still feel the same way now?

_____
_____
_____
_____
_____
_____
_____
_____
_____
_____

_____

Quotes

"A man cannot free himself from the past more easily than he can from his own body." ~André Maurois

"The one charm of the past is that it is the past." ~Oscar Wilde, *The Picture of Dorian Gray*

"The past is our definition. We may strive, with good reason, to escape it, or to escape what is bad in it, but we will escape it only by adding something better to it."
~Wendell Berry

"Bring the past only if you are going to build from it."
~Doménico Cieri Estrada

No matter what has happened, it has all existed to bring you to this moment. This is the moment you can choose to make everything new, this very moment.

Closure and Forgiveness

We carry around so much emotional baggage without even realizing it. There is anger you feel, moments of sadness that come over you, and you can't seem to figure out why. It's all because of closure you've never gotten at some point in your past. Someone may have betrayed you, or physically hurt you. A lover may have cheated on you, given you a sexually transmitted disease, or left you for someone else. You may have grown up seeing your father abuse your mother. You may have been abused, molested, or bullied as a child.

These feelings of anger and sadness still exist because

there was no closure. Closure tends to get misused in many situations. A lot of women use this word as an excuse to continue going back to Mr. No Good, but closure is the opposite of that. It's coming to a peaceful understanding of a person or experience, so that chapter can be closed and you can move on with your life.

Closure does not mean that you have to seek the person out who wronged you and talk to them directly. If you feel comfortable doing that, then that's fine. Do what works for you. Many find it easier to write a letter detailing all their feelings and things they never got to say. However you choose to do it, it is about getting things off your chest and heart, so that you no longer have to feel weighed down by it. Your feelings need to be addressed so that you can begin healing and moving past whatever it is. In the end, the burdens you've been carrying all this time should feel lifted.

Closure is a part of forgiveness, not just for others, but forgiveness for you. You can't begin to completely move on without forgiving someone, and you will continue to suffer until you forgive yourself. This may be an extremely emotional process, but take all the time you need. There may be many things and people you need to establish closure with, and this step is important in renewing yourself. This step isn't the easiest, and some may seek therapy for deeper rooted issues, or just the opportunity to speak to someone neutral. There is nothing wrong with seeking professional help to get you to the life and mind frame you would like to be in. After you close these

169

chapters, your heart will be free to start pursuing the happiness and life you desire and deserve.

Blaming vs. taking responsibility

When relationships don't work out, usually the blame game begins. It can be so easy to blame someone who's hurt you for the downfall of the relationship, and it just might be their actions that brought the relationship to an end. However, most women fail to accept responsibility for their part in toxic relationships. Yes, ladies, it's not all their fault.

I'm not saying Mr. No Good has any reason to cheat, abuse, or disrespect you in any way. His actions are based on his selfishness. However, Mr. No Good will only treat you as bad as you allow him to. No toxic behavior just starts suddenly, out of nowhere. There are almost always signs leading to toxic behavior. Most women tend to ignore the signs but then they're devastated when things get worse. This enabling plays a big part in Mr. No Good's lifestyle, because it gives him silent permission to continue doing wrong. You have to accept responsibility for looking the other way and giving no major consequence to Mr. No Good. If you refuse to accept responsibility for your part of enabling, you will continue on with the same enabling spirit into future relationships, which will continue to bring you dating woes.

It's not the end of the world. We all make mistakes, so you're definitely not alone. It's time to acknowledge that Mr. No Good treated you the way he did because he knew you wouldn't leave him. His actions got more disrespectful because he observed that you would allow it. The sooner you can admit that your enabling may have played a part in his toxic behavior, the quicker you can begin to work on changing your enabling ways. Recognizing your weakness is just as important as identifying his.

Remember: You can cry, give him the silent treatment, cut off sex, or whatever you choose when he's done wrong. However, when you choose to stay in the situation after he's wronged you, it completely cancels all of those "punishments" out. This behavior will drain you, and make you feel like you really did something that taught him a lesson, but the fact that you stayed (or came back to him) lets him know that his actions weren't too bad and that they were able to be dismissed. The greatest consequence would be to leave him and not look back. You're not teaching him a lesson by slapping his hand then staying with him.

Taking responsibility does not mean taking on an "I brought this on myself" way of thinking. You are not at fault for anyone's destructive behavior. You are only at fault for how much of the toxic behavior you choose to stick around and put up with. Own your decisions, own your mistakes, and move on to correct them.

Stop beating yourself up

Somewhere along the line we've all asked ourselves "How did I let myself get in this situation", or "How was I so blind to not see what kind of guy he was". Questions like these are asked so much. Even the smartest woman doesn't always see how badly damaged a person is as soon as they meet them. Sometimes it takes time for the warning signs to appear.

Stop beating yourself up over the decisions you made to get into a relationship with Mr. No Good. We cannot control who we develop feelings for. We can only choose our partners wisely, and hope for the best. Sure, you may have feelings for, or even love, Mr. No Good, but there is no law that states that you have to commit to or even be involved with someone that is no good for you. When you continue to beat yourself up for what you've been through, you continue to allow misery to remain in your life. You are not your mistakes and poor decisions.

You can choose to dwell on how things went wrong, and whose fault it was, or you can choose to move ahead with the knowledge to prevent it from happening again in the future. The choice is yours.

Forgiving yourself

You live and learn, it's true. Sometimes it's through other people's experiences, but usually it's through your own trial and error. In a world filled with people that are only human that are destined to make mistakes, we must learn to forgive not only others, but more importantly ourselves.

Pain, guilt, anger…..these are emotions that can eat away at you if forgiveness doesn't exist. Sometimes it's hard to look back at things we've done, or things that others have done to us without feeling these emotions. Whether you forgive and forget as many say, or forgive and never forget, you must first acquire the ability to forgive.

We are our own biggest critics, so it's natural that we can be much harder on ourselves than anyone else will be. With that being said, it can be difficult to heal and begin forgiving ourselves for some of the decisions we've made. But the process of forgiving has to start somewhere. There's no better time than now.

It's always been said that the first step to recovery is admitting you have a problem. The same works with forgiving. The first step to allowing forgiveness into your heart is to acknowledge that you have made mistakes. Making mistakes is common. We all make them. Understand that at the time you made those mistakes you may have been doing the best you could do, or the best you knew to do.

It's important to understand why forgiving yourself is needed. If you don't understand that the release is needed for you to grow, forgiving yourself won't be genuine. It will be forced and pointless. It is also important to understand that forgiving yourself will not change your past circumstances. Forgiveness will not undo anything, and it shouldn't be done for that reason. Forgiveness is for giving yourself peace of mind. It is to help you grow and blossom emotionally.

In forgiving yourself, don't make excuses for the things

that have happened. Own your mistakes, and learn from them.

<u>Forgiving others</u>

You shouldn't suffer for the rest of your life because of what someone else has done to you. Many women go through life bitter because a man (or men) has wronged them. No one's actions should have that much of an effect on you that it causes you to change your character and stunt your personal growth. You are giving that person in your past too much power. When you make the conscious decision to forgive others, you are releasing the control that person has had over your emotions, over your mind, over your wellbeing. Sometimes, getting the closure you want isn't possible. That doesn't mean stay hung up on what that person has done to you for the rest of your life. There may be times where forgiveness of others is the only closure you will have. You may not get that understanding of that person and why they did the things they did, but you can still clear your heart and mind by forgiving them anyway. You cannot afford to stay angry and full of resentment for the rest of your life.

How do you know that you've truly forgiven someone or yourself? You will know that it has happened when you feel less burdened, when those thoughts of your past mistakes aren't tugging at your conscience anymore, when you get a little more sleep at night without the things that have happened keeping you from relaxing as you should. Forgiveness doesn't mean forgetting the things you've been through, it simply means no longer letting them consume you. It means releasing all the negative emotions associated with it.

An effective way to help yourself forgive yourself and others is writing letters. It sounds cheesy, but it helps to get your emotions out on paper. The visual can be very powerful. Sometimes the person you want to forgive isn't available. Maybe they've passed away, or you don't have access to them. Maybe they're not ready to reconcile with you. Whatever the case, this forgiveness is for you, and sometimes getting it all down on paper can be therapeutic. This is also a good way to get your feelings out without the inconvenience of being interrupted. I'm sure you've had moments where you were prepared to say all that was on your mind, and you didn't get to or didn't remember because the person you were speaking to cut in to speak their piece. Writing can be very therapeutic. Some people I spoke to about how they've dealt with forgiveness have even written letters then burned them in order to visually experience the release. Others shared that they wrote letters and sent them to the people they were forgiving. One person shared with me that they wrote the letters of forgiveness, and stuck them inside their Bible to pray over them in the future. Do whatever works for you, as long as you're genuinely opening your heart to forgive.

- Who do you need to forgive?

- Are there any situations that weigh heavily on you?

- Have you felt anger, resentment, bitterness that you can't explain?
- Do your feelings towards those situations or people contribute to your views of relationships?

"What we don't recognize is that holding onto your resentment is like holding onto your breath. You'll soon start to suffocate."

-Deepak Chopra

"Forgiveness does not change the past, but it does enlarge the future."   -Paul Boese

"When you don't forgive those who've hurt you, you turn your back against your future. When you do forgive, you start walking forward."   -Tyler Perry

"Forgiving what we cannot forget creates a new way to remember. We change the memory of the past into a hope for our future." –Lewis Smedes

"The knowledge of the past stays with us. To let go is to release the images and emotions, the grudges and fears, the clinging and disappointments of the past that binds our spirit."-Jack Kornfield

Notes

_____

_____

_____

_____

_____

_____

_____

_____

_____

_____

_____

_____

_____

_____

_____

_____

Chapter 16-GettingYOU together

What's your vision?

All this time you've been a reactor to everything that you have experienced thus far, but it's time to renew your life, and start down the pathway towards your happiness. The transformation is long overdue, and now that you understand how your past was affecting you, you can finally regroup and start to create the life you desire.

What do you really want out of life? Now is a better time than ever to figure out what you want your life to consist of. What is your vision? What are your goals? Where do you see yourself in the near future and long term? It's important to design a vision for your life so that you'll have a blueprint to refer back to anytime you feel discouraged or that you've gotten off track.

Assignment: Write down everything you would like to accomplish and the type of man you want to be with. Be as honest as you can be. Remember, this is your vision, no one else's, so nothing is outlandish or unrealistic in your vision for your future. There are no limitations to this list. Be sure to add your goals for all aspects of your life, including finances, friendships, marriage, and any other thing you find significant in life.

I have left space in this book so that you could jot these things down. Feel free to write or type them on your own list that you can post anywhere in your home or work place as a daily reminder and motivator. This list has proven to be helpful to many people, including myself.

Goals

_____

_____

_____

_____

_____

_____

_____

_____

_____

_____

_____

_____

_____

_____

_____

_____

_____

_____

_____

_____

_____

_____

_____

_____

_____

_____

_____

_____

What do you think is standing in the way of who you are meant to be? We all have obstacles to overcome and sometimes we're not even sure what those obstacles are, because we don't really give it much thought. To become the best you, you have to first understand what holds you back.

What are your insecurities? What do you fear? What or who do you feel is holding you back from achieving goals? Make a list here. Remember to be completely honest.

_____

_____

_____

_____

_____

_____

_____

_____

_____

_____

_____

Modify what you can, minimize what you can't

We all have things that we may not like about ourselves, whether it is personality traits, financial situations, or physical features. It's common to have insecurities of some sort. While there are some things that can be easily changed, there are other things that aren't so easy to alter. The solution is not always easily found. However, it's up to you to make the best of your circumstances. To do this, try modifying the things you can change, and minimizing the things you can't control.

Sometimes we spend so much time focusing on our flaws and things we don't like, that we neglect the possibility of change. Stop dwelling on what's wrong, and start working on getting it right.

Here are examples of things that have somewhat simple solutions.

"I spend money easily."

"I eat when I'm upset."

"I've gained too much weight."

"I go out too much."

Those are just a few examples of things that have a simple solution. Yes, the solutions may require hard work, but if you really want to remix your life, you'll be willing to do everything you can to change those things you dislike about yourself. Before you can change your dating style, you must first get your own mind right.

Physical features are a great example of things that cannot be easily changed, yet it's one of the most common sources of insecurity. You may not like your teeth, your eyes, or your freckles. Many of us have at least one thing we don't like about ourselves, but everyone doesn't have the money to get cosmetic surgery.

In this case, the best thing to do is minimize as much as you can. This will make you feel more comfortable, even if the issue still remains. If you don't like your freckles or uneven skin tone, use foundation and concealer. If you hate your teeth, perfect a closed mouth smile. If you feel your eyes are set too far apart, try different makeup tips to make them appear closer. The important thing is that you're doing what you can with what you've got.

There are certain traits that we possess that aren't easily changed. The following is a list of examples.

I sleep with guys too quickly.

I lash out at others easily.

I don't trust anyone.

I judge others too much.

I let others take advantage of me.

I don't believe in myself.

These kinds of situations are based on internal issues. Although they are surfacing problems, they are a result of deeper rooted issues, and will take a lot of work to change. These changes do not happen overnight, but they are definitely worth working on.

You have made a list of what you feel is holding you back. Now it's time to make a list of the things you don't like about yourself. Be sure to include all aspects of your life. What do you dislike about your interactions with others (at work, on the street, with family, etc.)? What don't you like about how you look? What don't you like about your dating style? Write your list here, or on a piece of paper you can easily refer back to.

These lists are a great tool to refer back to whenever you feel that you're getting off track with your progression, or to give you a quick positive reminder of where you're at, where you've been, and where you're headed. I still make lists and go back to them to keep me pushing towards a better future. There is always room from improvement, no matter how great you become, and the reminder of where I used to be motivates me that much more to excel in life.

Turn insecurities into action

I want you to also list what you are currently doing to change or minimize the items on the list, as well as what you can do to change what you don't like. By listing both of these things, you can easily see the effort you are truly putting into getting to a better you, as well as the steps you need to take to get to that point. Sometimes a visual is just what we need to get on track. Turn your insecurities into action by focusing on what you can do to change the circumstances instead of the circumstance itself.

What I don't like about myself

_____
_____
_____
_____
_____
_____
_____
_____
_____
_____
  _____

What am I actually doing to change those things?

_____
_____
_____
_____
_____
_____

_____

_____

_____

What can I begin doing to help improve these things?

_____

_____

_____

_____

_____

_____

_____

_____

_____

_____

Remember: You are more than your circumstances. You will only begin to achieve the best you once you become proactive instead of reactive. Change starts here.

Part IV.

Starting Fresh

I love ME more Contract

I have loved, I have lost. I have been through the fire, and I admit I have not loved myself as I should in the past. However, my past did not break me. It did not defeat me. I am stronger. I am smarter. I am a survivor of heart ache, and my past will not destroy my future. I deserve love. I deserve real love. I deserve happiness. I deserve a life that is lived to the fullest.

From this point on, I refuse to settle for anything or anyone that makes me unhappy. I refuse to give my time, attention, and heart to anyone that makes me feel anything less than my best. I will give no energy to anyone or anything that makes me feel insignificant or insecure. This time around I will love me more. From this moment on, I will choose happiness over unhealthy. No longer will I struggle with loving myself, and no longer will I tolerate toxic people or relationships.

Signature: _____ Date:_____

I wrote that message when I was at a very low place in a toxic relationship. I had been lied to over and over, verbally abused, and cheated on many times. I was at my breaking point. I knew I should've been gone already, but I didn't love myself enough to say "enough is enough". It wasn't until I sat down and wrote these simple, yet powerful words that I began to believe that I deserved better than what I was settling for. I wrote this message and stuck it in my Bible so that no one could find it. Every morning, I would say my prayers, and start my day by reading that message. The more I said those words aloud, the more I believed in them.

Today, I still read that message, not as a reminder, but as a declaration. It serves as a great ego boost, and starts my day off with a big smile. I share this message with you so that you can also be empowered. Read this message as much as you want. Carry it around with you as a reminder in times when your confidence level isn't where it needs to be. I hope that it will be as powerful of a message to you as it was, and still is, to me.

NOTES

Chapter 17-The next step

Congratulations! You've made it to the other side if you're reading this section. You are finally ready to introduce the world to a new and improved you. Doesn't it feel good to be renewed and reinvented? You deserve this, be excited! True happiness can be yours now that you know what it means and how it feels to love yourself. You've put in the work. Now it's time to take your new outlook on relationships and confidence for a test drive. Are you ready? Of course you are!

Do you want "the good life" or a good life?

What do you think about when you hear the phrase "the good life"? Surely, many have nodded their head to Kanye West's hit song which is titled just the same. But what does it mean to you? I interviewed 200 women over a year's time and almost all of the answers to this question contained superficial words. The most common answers included the following:

- Fame
- Luxury
- Famous friends
- Wealth
- Yachts
- mansions

190

It seems the good life to most is a glamorous one, where everyone is filthy rich and well known. In the same interviews, I changed one word, and asked the ladies what does it mean to have a good life. Answers were completely different. They included the following:

- Love
- Happiness
- Marriage
- A great job
- Loyal friends
- Morals
- Stability

It was amazing how much of a difference was made when "the" was replaced with "a". Often we tend to let society trick us into thinking we should be striving for "the good life", instead of a good life. Sure, it's nice to have everything we want, along with popularity, but this superficial idea of a successful life will not be enough to give you the ultimate happiness you'd have in just living a good life. Material things can only make you happy for so long before you begin longing for a life of purpose instead of a life of luxury. Which life will you choose?

Hitting life's curveballs

There will be days that aren't so great. It doesn't matter how much you've evolved. Sucky days exist for all of us. No one ever said life would be perfect even in learning to love yourself. Some days you may still feel down and out.

On days like those, think about how far you've come. Think about the unhappiness you had the strength to leave behind you. When life decides to throw those curveballs, step up to the plate and smash them out of the ball park. Don't waste anymore energy on negative thoughts.

Think of your setbacks as an opportunity to point you in another direction. We are usually quick to worry and pout, instead of wondering what we can make out of the situation at hand.

In the past, there was a time when everything that can go wrong went wrong. I was in between jobs, and my license got suspended due to not being able to pay my traffic tickets. I found another job, which excited me because I had just gotten a new car and new place right before I got laid off. This new job would allow me to continue paying for everything I had just accumulated. But when it rains, it pours.

On the way to my new job, a cop pulled me over to let me know one of my lights had blown out. That stop ended up getting my license plate taken due to my suspended license, and not only did it give me more tickets to pay, but it also stopped me from having reliable transportation to get to work.

Things only went downhill from there. Without a license plate I couldn't drive my car to get to work. This resulted in not having paychecks to pay rent or bills. My electricity and water got turned off, and my car was added to the repossession list, on top of being evicted from my new place. One thing after another caused my life to start falling apart.

During this time I was at a low place, physically, emotionally, and psychologically. I was so depressed and felt that most of those who cared about me weren't there for me when I needed them the most. The whole situation was enough to break even the strongest person. Here I was, living in a place with no electricity, no water, no money, no phone, and having to walk miles to shower and get water. I couldn't even afford food, so I was eating every few days. I did nothing but write, pray, and walk to keep peace of mind.

I never gave up on life. I refused to lie down and let my circumstances consume me. I continued to pray and come up with solutions to get out of the mess that I had gotten into. Instead of complaining, I looked at the walking as a way to lose weight and stay healthy. I continued to post my resume and look for jobs at the nearest college campus, and I even helped others revise their resumes during this time. The downtime due to being laid off was viewed as a way to finally have time to focus on my writing. Most of this book was finished during this time in my life.

I had to learn quickly that life can suck, but you have to keep a positive mindset and make the best of what you're working with. It was such a horrible situation that I would never want to end up in again, but it was a valuable learning experience that I will always be grateful for. Know that you can still flourish even in your times of trouble, or at rock bottom.

Laying the foundation

You've learned so much about yourself and the things you want in life throughout your reading of this book. You know what Mr. No Good looks like, and now it's time to start establishing what kind of guy and relationship you prefer.

By this time, you should be well acquainted with the things you like and dislike in a guy. You have had your share of Mr. No Goods, and know now what you will and will not tolerate. By understanding these things, you are fool proofing your plan to never settle for a toxic relationship again.

Use this space to write down all the qualities you desire in a guy. Be as detailed as you want to be, because this will be a go-to list for your future dates. What kinds of things do guys do that make you smile? Is their clothing style a factor? List it. Is a man with kids okay? Write that down. This is all about what you want in a guy. This is what you want out of a relationship.

What are your deal breakers? You've dealt with Mr. No Good enough to be able to pinpoint the things you don't like. What won't you tolerate in your future relationships? What behaviors and traits will turn you off upon first meeting a guy? Write them down. This list will serve as a daily reminder of the road you are too good to travel back down.

_____

_____

_____

_____

_____

_____

_____

_____

_____

_____

_____

_____

_____

_____

_____

_____

_____

_____

_____

_____

_____

_____

_____

_____

_____

_____

_____

_____

Get over perfection

We've all been taught the phrase "nobody's perfect", yet we still tend to live our lives expecting perfection in ourselves and others. This is extremely prevalent in relationships, where many long for that perfect man that doesn't exist. Our longing for perfection breeds extremely high and unrealistic expectations, which result in feeling like no guy is good enough. Every guy we meet has some kind of deal breaker, and then dating becomes a disappointing chore instead of a fun one.

Let go of the image you have of the perfect man. Be reasonable. If we have problems ourselves, how can we expect others not to? It is okay to desire certain traits in a man, but don't get caught up in expecting your potential man to have no issues. Mr. Right will not always be drop dead gorgeous with great credit, no kids, extremely family oriented, and loaded with cash. He doesn't have to be perfect to be perfect for you. This doesn't mean lower your standards and settle for Mr. No Good. You know how to spot him and steer clear now. But just maybe……you're not having any luck because you're setting unrealistically high standards.

We all want someone to treat us with respect, be loyal, and shower us with love and affection. That guy doesn't always come with a body of a Greek god, or 6'5" frame. He may not be a doctor or professional athlete, but he has a decent job that gets the bills paid. He may not have Bradley Cooper or Lamman Rucker's beautiful face, but he may have a heart of gold and great intentions. Don't shut Mr. Right out searching for a gorgeous surface, and don't let Mr. No Good in just because he's great eye candy.

During my years of research, I've encountered many men that complain about being overlooked by most women. The common complaint was that women ignore them because they're not flashy enough or don't drive expensive cars. These men had great backgrounds, good jobs, and were searching for a woman that they could treat like a queen. Most of them were very handsome, and took great care of themselves. However, the buzz around them wasn't big enough for women to give them a second glance.

Pay attention to what draws you to a man. Sure, appearance is important, but don't let it stop you from getting to know a potentially good mate. Besides, do you really want a man ignoring or rejecting you because you don't have Louboutins on, or because you're not driving a Mercedes Benz? If you don't want to be judged superficially, treat others the same.

When dealing with views on perfection, you should

also acknowledge your own feelings about being perfect. We get so caught up in how others view us that it begins to make us judge ourselves harder than we should. You don't have to be perfect to gain happiness. The important thing is to find someone that accepts and loves you, flaws and all.

I love Beyonce's song "Flaws and All" because it speaks of all her insecurities and not-so-perfect qualities, something we all can relate to. The beauty of it all is that someone still loves her with all that is wrong, and it makes her love him even more. You can have this kind of unconditional love too, but you must first accept two things:

1. You were not created to be perfect.
2. You don't have to be.

Even with your imperfections, you are worthy of love. You are worthy of happiness. You are worthy of respect. Don't sell yourself short by feeling that you're not good enough. You never know, the very things you dislike about yourself could be the very things someone may love about you. Stop zooming in on what's wrong with you, and emphasize what you like about yourself. Remember, change what you can and minimize what you can't. Get comfortable with the fact that you aren't meant to be perfect, and get confident that you're still worthy of happiness.

No negativity allowed

Many women tend to become bitter after being in toxic relationships. This anger usually stems from low self concept, not just the behavior of Mr. No Good itself. This bitterness can cause major negativity and pessimistic views on dating and relationships. Don't let destructive relationships turn you bitter. Take them as an opportunity for you to know and do better.

If you want to successfully date, you must first drop all the negative beliefs about men. Don't let your past experience hinder you from recognizing a good man when you meet one. Negative thinking is an unattractive trait, and it can cause others to focus more on your pessimism instead of your great qualities.

All men aren't dogs. Just because you've dated your fair share of no good men doesn't mean that they are all the same. All men are not the same, and this outlook will only discourage you, and keep you in a bitter mind state. Keep an open mind. Don't assume every guy you meet will eventually hurt you. You are now well acquainted with Mr. No Good's ways, so it should be easier to spot the red flags. Give the guys you meet a fair chance. It's not right that someone new has to pay for what someone in your past has done.

Every guy won't mess up. Don't give up on a guy before he's even had a fair chance. Often we assume that a guy has disguised intentions before we even get to really feel them out. This is due to not letting go of your past.

That is why Part 3 of this book is so important. Without fully letting go, we can't change our mind frame. Without changing our mind set, we cannot grow. There's no way you can change your behavior without first changing the way you think.

Give yourself some credit. Don't go into your renewed life expecting to mess up. Yes, you will make mistakes. No, everything won't always flow like you want it to. However, don't let fear of failing stop from the chance of succeeding. You can't hit a homerun if you never step up to the plate to even take a swing. You've accomplished greatness just in learning your worth, and having the courage to stop settling. Take a chance on happiness, and expect great results. You have to first believe in yourself and know your worth, so that others can know it too.

Push the boundaries

Aren't you tired of living within your comfort zone? Aren't you exhausted with feeling like you've hit the dead end of relationships? It's time to step out of that box you've confined yourself to. You've been in that box way too long.

We all have limits, and we do our best to stick within them. However, if we never push the boundaries we create, as well as the ones that we feel are created for us, then we never really progress. If your dating views remain the same as they were during your toxic relationships, you will never experience the growth you need to achieve true happiness. This is why pushing the boundaries is so important.

You weren't meant to stay stagnant in the world of dating and relationships. You are more than the box you're keeping yourself in. Push past the point in your life you have gotten to, and dive into the happiness you deserve. You will never know your true potential until you try shooting for a higher goal. Go for above and beyond, instead of just settling for good enough. It's what pushing the boundaries is about.

What does this mean for you in the dating world? Try new things. Try a new mind set. Create a new look for yourself. Pushing the boundaries is all about trying something different than what you're used to. It's about realizing what doesn't work for you, and taking a chance on what will. There is beauty in reinvention. Give the guy a chance you always chat with at the gym. Don't be afraid to give out your number if you're interested in someone. Go on a date to a place you've never tried before. Take chances without taking away from your standards. You owe it to yourself to try new things that can lead to your ultimate happiness.

NOTES

_____

_____

_____

_____

_____

_____

_____

_____

Ready, Set, Date!

Congratulations! Hopefully this book has helped you undergo a major transformation in love and life. You've learned about Mr. No Good, and gained the courage to let go of the men in your life who don't treat you like you deserve to be treated. More importantly, you have learned the importance of loving yourself enough to realize when you deserve better.

The insecurities, doubt, and pain have been lifted. No longer should you feel that you deserve Mr. No Good. No longer will he be able to take control of your happiness. Use your story as a lesson. Use your past pain as motivation to gain ultimate happiness. Give yourself permission to date again. After all, you deserve the best love has to offer. Good luck!

www.ingramcontent.com/pod-product-compliance
Lightning Source LLC
LaVergne TN
LVHW052024080426
835513LV00018B/2140